ירושלים

The LION of JUDAH

RABBI KIRT A. SCHNEIDER

CHARISMA
HOUSE

after publication. Further, the publisher does not have any control over and does not assume any responsibility for author or third-party websites or their content.

18 19 20 21 22 — 987654321
Printed in the United States of America

Contents

Part I
Why Judaism and Christianity Separated

Part II
How Jesus Completes
Biblical Judaism

ACKNOWLEDGMENTS

To a degree, we are all products of those around us who have invested into our lives. God often uses others to impart something of Himself to us. With this in mind, I want to thank my parents, my wife and children, my first Messianic Bible teachers, and the many others who have poured into my life and taught me much about the Lord. For this book in particular, I also want to acknowledge my good friend and editor, Marcus Yoars, for helping me to bring this book, *The Lion of Judah*, to the forefront!

INTRODUCTION

THE LORD IS ONE, SO WHAT HAPPENED TO HIS PEOPLE?

I SPENT THE FIRST ten years of my life in Beachwood, Ohio, a suburb of Cleveland with the second-highest concentration of Jewish people outside Israel. Ninety percent of Beachwood's residents are Jewish, so seeing a Gentile in our community was rare.[1] In fact, everywhere you turned, you could find evidence of just how Jewish the environment was. Almost all the families in my neighborhood had names such as Rosenthal, Levine, Katz, Feinberg, Schwartz, Berg, and Stein. Most children my age attended Hebrew school three days a week after regular school had ended. Public schools closed on Rosh Hashanah (the Jewish new year) and Yom Kippur (the Day of Atonement), and on those days it seemed as if the whole community was in temple.

Although my family moved to Pepper Pike, another Cleveland suburb, when I was in the sixth grade, I continued attending Hebrew school. My family remained heavily involved with the Jewish community. I attended synagogue not only for Hebrew school but also every year on Rosh Hashanah and Yom Kippur. In the seventh grade I was bar mitzvahed in a conservative synagogue, and by that time it was clear to me that I was to be proud of my heritage.

I remember getting this sense particularly during services in temple, when the rabbi would pray the Shema, the ancient prayer found in Deuteronomy 6 that has become the centerpiece of Jewish belief and declaration. The Shema begins with:

Sh'ma Yisra'el! Adonai Eloheinu, Adonai echad.

—DEUTERONOMY 6:4, CJB

1

Hear, O Israel: The LORD is our God. The LORD is one!
—DEUTERONOMY 6:4

The problem, however, was that God wasn't really part of the picture, nor did He seem to be intimately "ours." Although we were called God's chosen people, no one around me ever actually talked *about* Him, much less referred to Him in a personal way.[2] The people I knew referred to Him as Adonai (the Hebrew word meaning "Lord"), but they never actually discussed who He was. Through all my early years I never heard anything about knowing God or having a relationship with Him.

A personal God was far removed from my experience in Beachwood and Pepper Pike. He was somewhere out there. At one point in history He had interacted with my ancestors, but that was long, long ago—so far back that any stories about Him felt more like fairy tales than actual accounts.

When I began attending Hebrew school at Park Synagogue, one of Cleveland's largest conservative synagogues, I again heard the Shema and its other parts, including:

V'ahav'ta eit Adonai Elohekha b'khol l'vav'kha uv'khol naf'sh'kha uv'khol m'odekha.[3]

And you shall love the LORD your God with all your heart and with all your soul and with all your might.
—DEUTERONOMY 6:5

As moving as these words sound, they were almost meaningless to me since I still knew nothing about God's love for me or His desire to be involved in my life. My mother drove me three days a week from regular school to Hebrew school, where I learned how to read and write Hebrew. There I memorized Hebrew prayers and was taught about my Jewish heritage, culture, and customs.

I absolutely dreaded it. In fact, I became so bored with Hebrew school that often I feigned walking into the school building and, after my mother drove off, went across the parking lot to sit under a tree in a secluded wooded area. My playing hooky eventually cost me, and I spent that summer with a private tutor while all my friends were out having fun. Yet even in this one-on-one setting where I was to learn about what it meant to be Jewish—part of a people formed out of covenant with God—I don't remember even once my teacher telling me about a god whom I could be close with or who loved me.

Indeed, most of my religious instruction centered exclusively on preparation for my bar mitzvah. This would be the pinnacle of my "Jewishness," when, at age thirteen, I was to become a "son of [the] commandment" (the literal translation of *bar mitzvah*). In transitioning from boyhood to manhood, I was to be held morally responsible before God and obey His commandments (*mitzvot*). But what kind of God was this?

I prepared for my bar mitzvah by memorizing the part of the Torah reading assigned to me for that day. My parents hired a tutor to help me with this, and I listened endlessly to an audio recording of my part. Yet as the big event neared, the words of the Hebrew Bible still never sank in but were simply words I needed to mouth to pass the test. I was participating in our Jewish culture but remained unmoved in a practical, spiritual sense.

END OF THE ROAD

My bar mitzvah lived up to its hype. When the day finally arrived, I was both excited and nervous. I had studied countless hours and worked hard on what I would do in the ceremony, yet I just wanted to get through it so I could have fun. During my bar mitzvah I recited some Hebrew prayers, read my portion of the Torah and the Hebrew prophets, listened to the rabbi, and received my tefillin (two small boxes containing portions of the Torah that are tied to the hand, arm, and forehead). I will never forget the sense of accomplishment once everything was done. Yet what I remember most was the party afterward.

This was no ordinary party. It took place at a beautiful banquet facility called The Executive Club. The celebration was so grand my parents hired two separate bands for the music—one for the adults and another for the children. Out of the hundreds of family members, classmates, and friends who came, I was particularly interested in a girl named Janice, whom I especially liked. As the band was playing, I made my big move and asked Janice to dance with me. What a sight it must have been to see my adolescent, five-foot frame moving out of step with her five-foot-seven body in an awkward slow dance. Standing so close to her, I was, I thought, in love.

It was a day I will never forget, yet it officially ended my Jewish education. I still wasn't sure why my bloodline defined so much in my life and set me apart in so many ways.

Sadly most Jewish people I know share a similar story. Our formal Jewish education concludes when the bar mitzvah party is over, and we are left with far more questions than answers about God, life, our Jewish identity, and everything in between. Though the deeper inquiries linger as we age—What makes us so special? What role do we play in the world? Why are we hated so much?—they often get buried under our customs, traditions, history, and expectations. For many Jews, these cultural elements become the essence of what it means to be Jewish rather than anything related to the God who made us Jewish in the first place. We get bar mitzvahed (or bat mitzvahed for girls) and celebrate Passover, Rosh Hashanah, Yom Kippur, Chanukah, and perhaps a few other Jewish holidays, but we often don't understand what these actually mean or why we do them. Our grandparents did them, and their grandparents, and theirs also...so we figure we should as well. We do these things because, well, we are Jewish, and that's just how it is.

With such strong traditions guiding countless generations, it is no wonder that the Jewish identity today is based more upon our heritage, customs, being part of the Jewish community, and what we do rather than upon our relationship with God. Many Jews I know do not understand that they can have a personal relationship with God. This is one of the reasons we are considered the "least religious" among all peoples and that so many of us claim to not even believe God exists.[4]

For those who still believe He does exist, we are divided. To truly understand the Jewish culture today, you must realize that Judaism as a religion is not unified. Different expressions of Judaism are often in conflict with each other. Generally the three main expressions of the Jewish religion are referred to as Reform Judaism, Conservative Judaism, and Orthodox Judaism. The Reform expression is the least religious, focusing primarily on social issues. Reform Jews believe much of the Torah is outdated and that each generation has the right to determine which laws are most relevant and essential to its age. Orthodox Jews take the opposite approach and are known for their strict adherence to Jewish law—both the Torah and the Jewish traditions passed along through rabbinic authorities. Meanwhile, Conservative Jews straddle the line between the modernity of Reform Judaism and the tradition of Orthodox Judaism. They adhere to many of the Torah's laws, including keeping kosher, yet also allow for certain innovations, such as driving to synagogue on Shabbat.

Within these three main streams of Judaism are other groups, all of which differ slightly in their beliefs and practices. Yet one thing that all three major expressions agree upon is that Jesus is not the Son of God or the Messiah.

THE GREAT DIVIDE

Ah, Jesus.

Ask any Jew what the difference is between Judaism and Christianity, and he will quickly point to Jesus. Simply put, one believes He is God, and the other doesn't. One honors Him as the long-awaited Messiah—"God with us" in flesh—while the other still awaits a promised Savior.

Of course, the differences between Jews and Christians go beyond who we say Jesus is or was. Much of this book will delve into these other dividing issues, many of which have become the cultural elements Jews cling to as part of their Jewishness. But at the heart of true Jewish identity, Jesus is still a factor, for He is either the ultimate fulfillment or the ultimate fraud.

It is ironic: Jesus was born as a Jew, lived as a Jew, died as a Jew, and was originally followed only by Jews, and yet for two thousand years Jews have distanced themselves from Him more adamantly than any other group on earth. As we will look at in a later chapter, the man who shaped history lived entirely in a Jewish context and even stated that He was sent "only to the lost sheep of the house of Israel" (Matt. 15:24), and yet that house generally either despises Him and refuses to call Him one of their own or begrudgingly refers to Him as a good moral teacher who happened to be Jewish. Meanwhile, since Jesus' death—under a sign that read "King of the Jews," no less—billions of Gentiles have claimed this Jewish man as their Lord and Savior.

Clearly Jesus, the Jew, is a link—*the* link, to be more precise—between Jews and Christians. He is the common denominator, and yet whether you see Him as the problem or answer—as the distortion or fulfillment of God's Word—is determined by on which side of the fence you stand.

When you really think about it, however, why is there a fence in the first place? Why did Judaism and Christianity become separate if one originated entirely from the other? If Jews and Christians both believe in the same God—the one Lord and one God of the Shema—why is there such division? Why is history littered with deathly accounts of this division, from the early Jewish persecution of Christ followers to the Christian Crusades' mass slaughtering of Jews in the name of a Jewish Jesus?

The division is still evident today. Recent surveys reveal that Jews in America feel the coldest toward evangelical Christians—even more than toward Muslims or atheists—despite Evangelicals having been the most supportive group of Jews in recent years.[5] Meanwhile, global anti-Semitism continues to rise. Studies prove that the number of reported incidents targeting Jews (vandalisms, bomb threats, instances of harassment, etc.) has risen sharply throughout the world.[6] Equally disconcerting is that many of these incidents have occurred in nations where the largest percentage of citizens call themselves Christian. Even though Christianity and Judaism come from the same place—twin religions birthed from the same womb, as some historians describe them[7]—clearly there is a serious split between them, one that has existed for almost two thousand years. But why?

THE FULFILLMENT

Near the beginning of Jesus' most famous sermon He made a profound statement that is imperative for both Christians and Jews to consider today. At the time, Jesus had kicked off His ministry with a bang. His powerful preaching, teaching, and healing were already beginning to draw massive crowds from miles and miles away—so much so that Matthew says, "His fame went throughout all Syria" (4:24). I imagine, then, that whispers and rumors were already starting to swirl: "This man is not normal—He speaks with a higher authority, and He walks with supernatural power. Could it be possible? Could He be the Promised One?"

One day, with the crowds still surrounding Him, Jesus walked up to the top of a mountain, sat down, and began teaching His disciples, as any rabbi would do. In His Sermon on the Mount, Jesus told them about a heavenly kingdom where the merciful, pure in heart, and meek are actually considered blessed. He challenged His followers to consider themselves fortunate when they are persecuted. And He called these same people the salt and light of the world.

These are often seen as the headlines from Jesus' message that day. But what He had to say next was maybe one of the most important statements He could have made, and it still resounds with great significance two thousand years later:

> Do not think that I have come to abolish the Law or the Prophets. I have not come to abolish, but to fulfill.
>
> —MATTHEW 5:17

Jesus had no need to make this statement at the time. No one seemed to be accusing Him of throwing out the commandments of the Torah or any other parts of the Hebrew Bible. Yet not only did

He know those accusations would come soon enough, but He also knew how crucial it was for all humanity to know that He *fulfilled* every command God gave His people.

The world would be a different place if Jesus had not fulfilled but instead done away with all that God had previously established. Ultimately it would have made the Jewish people and their God-given laws irrelevant. Yet the Jews were God's chosen people, the very means through which He desired to bless the world and reveal Himself to all nations. God had given the Law and the Prophets (meaning the entire Hebrew Bible) to the Jewish people as a standard by which they were to live so that they would be a separated, consecrated, holy nation, a "kingdom of priests" unto Him—a living symbol of His covenant to the world (Exod. 19:6). If Jesus had come to abolish the Law, then it would render all that meaningless. But Christ did the opposite, which meant the Jewish identity was now ultimately found *through* Him! He was the perfect Jew, the essence of what it meant to be Jewish. And by fulfilling every single command and prophecy, Jesus became the rightful head of this chosen people.

This is why Jesus is called the Lion of Judah in the Book of Revelation, and why that name will have such power through all eternity. In John's vision of a day to come, Jesus is the only One able to open the scroll that releases a time of both judgment and redemption for all creation. Yet it is fascinating that of all the titles Jesus is given at this pinnacle moment in history, as described in the Book of Revelation, He is called the "Lion of the tribe of Judah":

> And I saw a strong angel proclaiming with a loud voice, "Who is worthy to open the scroll and to break its seals?" But no one in heaven or on earth or under the earth was able to open the scroll or to look in it. I began to weep loudly, because no one was found worthy to open and read the scroll, or to look in it. Then one of the elders said to me, "Do not weep. Look! The *Lion of the tribe of Judah*, the Root

of David, has triumphed. He is able to open the scroll and
to loose its seven seals."

—REVELATION 5:2–5, EMPHASIS ADDED

The Lord will reign as the rightful king of the Jewish people and
indeed over every "tribe" on earth. In Israel's history the tribe of
Judah was traditionally the royal tribe from which kings came. King
David was from the line of Judah, and God promised that "David
shall never lack a man to sit on the throne of the house of Israel" and
that He would "establish his royal throne forever" (Jer. 33:17; 2 Sam.
7:13). The tribe of Judah, therefore, carried a royal bloodline—it was
the ultimate standard of "Jewishness." It is not by chance that Jesus
came from this same tribe and will be continually associated with it
for all time.

But why is He called the *Lion* of Judah? The tribe's ancient symbol of a lion dates back to when Jacob blessed his fourth son and
called him a lion whose "brothers shall praise" him and who will rule
with a scepter that "shall not depart...until Shiloh comes; and to
him will be the obedience of the people" (Gen. 49:8–10). Jacob spoke
these words almost two thousand years before Jesus was born, which
means his Messianic blessing remained unfulfilled until Christ.

Many of those who listened to Jesus' Sermon on the Mount
would have been aware of this blessing as well as countless other passages throughout the Hebrew Bible. So when Jesus said He came not
"to abolish the Law or the Prophets...but to fulfill" them, He most
certainly would have captured their attention (Matt. 5:17). He was
pronouncing His absolute relevance to the Jewish people, their Bible,
and their way of life. He was declaring Himself the completion of
Judaism itself—something Israel's religious leaders have passionately
denied ever since. Yet as we will examine throughout this book, Judaism is incomplete without Jesus. He is the ultimate fulfillment of
everything it means to be Jewish—the Law, the Prophets, even the
customs and traditions.

Can you begin to see how tragic it is that the people who have historically rejected Jesus the most are the very people He represents?

Jesus is not just the "Christian" Savior; He is the Lion of Judah, birthed from the royal bloodline of Jews. He is the Jews' Jew, to put it crudely. And He is returning to "draw all people"—Jews and Gentiles—to Himself (John 12:32, NIV).

I have titled this book *The Lion of Judah* because in it we will examine how Jesus, as the Lion of Judah, is the aim of both the Hebrew Bible (what most believers call the Old Testament) and the New Testament. In the following pages we will see how Jesus completes and fulfills the entire Bible for both Jews and Christians. Given that Jesus came to fulfill the Hebrew Bible, you would think the Jewish people would recognize all the different ways He completes their faith, and yet this is obviously not the case today or throughout history. Throughout the following chapters you will better understand why Israel has not recognized Jesus as the Lion of Judah and its promised Messiah, and ultimately how this has caused such separation between Judaism and Christianity.

My prayer is that you do not merely gain information from this book, though it contains much. No, my ultimate hope is that you receive greater revelation of who Jesus is and how magnificently He has fulfilled every word in the Bible—the Law, Prophets, and more. The Lion of Judah is the rightful Lord and King of all people—Jews, Christians, Muslims, Buddhists, Sikhs, atheists…of *all* creation. As you see Him from such a place of revelation, I pray that you can know Him in a deeper way than ever before. May these pages lead you closer to Him!

CHAPTER 1

REDISCOVERING
ANCIENT TREASURES

I WAS TWENTY YEARS old when I saw Jesus for the first time. Having grown up in a tight-knit Jewish community, I cannot remember ever hearing His name mentioned during my upbringing. This made my encounter with Him even more radical and profound.

I saw Him on a summer night in August 1978, when I suddenly awoke from my sleep in a state that I would describe as conscious awareness. I was aware that I was not sleeping and that something was going on. Even though I had never even thought about the concept of having a vision, this is exactly what I experienced. Jesus appeared to me—in full color. I could see the terrain in which the cross He hung upon was staked. As this scene appeared to me, a ray of red light beamed down on Jesus' head from the sky straight above Him. When I saw the light, I knew it was from God because it was piercing through the heavens. Although I knew nothing about Jesus, had never read the New Testament, and, in fact, had never even considered Him, I knew in an instant that God was showing me that Jesus was the way to Him. This was at a point in my life when I was lost and searching for meaning and identity. Yet in that moment I knew God had revealed the answer to what I was seeking.

That experience began a journey of following Jesus that continues to this day. It opened up a whole new world for me, as did the words of the Bible, which I began to devour as a new believer in *Yeshua HaMashiach* (Hebrew for "Jesus the Messiah"). Through the Scriptures I discovered that God *was* a personal God who wanted to be intimately involved with every aspect of my life, and that His Son, Yeshua, was living proof of His love for me. God was revealing more and more of Himself to me everywhere I turned.

The year after I was saved, I remember visiting a church with a friend of mine, where we joined a few hundred other believers to worship God. As a brand-new Christian, I was eager to receive as much Bible teaching as I could, and when the preacher began his sermon, I hung on his every word. Yet what I heard that day did not line up with what I had been reading in the Bible. The preacher declared that God had done all He could, and because His work was finished through Jesus' dying on the cross, it was now up to us to complete our salvation. The problem, the preacher passionately stated, was that mankind's free will was in the way and continued to thwart God's purposes. Indeed, the God this preacher portrayed was frustrated and impotent, as if He were up in the sky with His hands tied behind His back. God wanted to do something but could not because people would not let Him. It seemed everything, including the outcome of the universe, was dependent on us.

As I listened to this man, something rose up in me that strongly rejected his portrayal of a weak and frustrated God. After the service I went with my friend to talk with the preacher, and I challenged him on his theology regarding God's sovereignty, pointing out passages of Scripture such as Romans 9, which deals with God's sovereign election of people to bring about His divine purposes for salvation. Unfortunately the response I received from the preacher was anything but open. Not long into our conversation he turned to my friend and abruptly said of me, "This guy refuses to read his Bible!"

I was taken aback; after all, I was still only twenty-one years old and a new believer. Yet the Bible I read did not present such an incapacitated God. He was sovereign, which meant He ruled over all things, had control over all things, and was uncontained in His power. As I later began to think about why this man and I had such a different understanding of who God is—and, in particular, how sovereign He is—I realized that the answer lay in my Jewish upbringing. In Judaism, God is Adon Olam, which means "master of the universe." Although the Jewish culture I was raised in did not talk about Adon Olam as a personal God, I still grew up with an internal concept of God's limitless power. Even if I thought He was far away, God was still sovereign. This is because Judaism places a high emphasis on God's sovereignty and power, whereas in some Christian circles humanity's free will is highlighted more.

Often Christians will base their entire belief system solely on New Testament principles without ever mining the truths of God found in the Old Testament. After that experience at the church I began to recognize that when we, as Christians, are not rooted in the Old Testament *as well as* the New Testament, we can develop a distorted view of who God is. As was the case with this preacher, we can often neglect God's sovereignty, which extends throughout the entire Bible. In the Book of Daniel, for example, King Nebuchadnezzar learned that his stubborn will could not ultimately prevail against an all-powerful God, and as he came to the end of his life, he declared that God "does according to His will in the army of heaven and among the inhabitants of the earth. And no one can stay His hand or say to Him, 'What have you done?'" (4:35).

God is not just sovereign; there are many other aspects of His nature revealed in the Old Testament. The Old Testament is God's self-revelation, as is the New Testament. They are not two separate books; the Bible is one progressive revelation of who God is. Unfortunately many Christians today treat the Old and New Testaments as two completely different books, as if there were no link between them and as if one were completely irrelevant to the other. Nothing could be further from the truth! In fact, every book of the Tanakh, or what Gentile believers know as the Old Testament, is intricately linked to the B'rit Hadashah (the New Testament). My prayer is that through the pages of this book you will discover how the Old and New Testaments fit together like a hand and a glove.

For example, it is not by chance that the very first verse of the New Testament begins by reaching back into Genesis of the Old Testament. Matthew 1:1 starts with, "The book of the genealogy of Jesus Christ, the Son of David, the son of Abraham," and then draws a detailed family tree of Jesus that stretches back forty-two generations. For most modern Christians, the meaning of this long list of "begots" is usually lost amid a stream of tongue-twisting names. For a Jew, however, anyone whose bloodline extends to patriarchs such as David, Jacob, Isaac, and Abraham warrants attention. For Jewish people both today and thousands of years ago, heritage—whom you come from—means everything. So it is no fluke that the main common denominator between the Old and New Testaments—Jesus the Messiah—is immediately linked through His heritage to some of Jewish history's most important people.

It is also not by chance that Jesus' genealogy connects Him to each of the elements of the Tanakh, which is the Hebrew Bible. The Tanakh is made up of three parts: the Torah (written by Moses), Nevi'im (meaning "prophets"), and Ketuvim ("writings," such as Psalms). Jesus specifically mentioned these three parts when He spoke of how He fulfilled all three: "These are the words which I spoke to you while I was still with you, that all things must be fulfilled which were written in *the Law of Moses* and in *the Prophets* and in *the Psalms* concerning Me" (Luke 24:44, emphasis added). In other words, Jesus was saying that the writings in all three sections of the Hebrew Bible point to Him. When we view God's Word in this way, as one book written by the one true God, we can unveil the deeper revelations He desires for us to gain.

SPIRITUAL SCHIZOPHRENIA

The good news is that as we discover the timeless threads connecting the Old and New Testaments, our passion for God increases. The bad news, however, is that I see many people missing out on this today and instead reading the Bible with spiritual schizophrenia. They think God has split-personality disorder and that He is different in the Old Testament than in the New Testament. Based on their distorted conclusion, the God of the Old Testament is a harsh lawgiver, full of anger and quick to judge, while the God of the New Testament is a loving Father who is so nice and merciful that He overlooks any sin.

This distorted view of God feeds a distorted view of Scripture, which then feeds back into the first. When people see God as inconsistent and divided, it cannot help but affect how they see His Word. As a result, they view the Bible as split in the same way. Left of Matthew is all about law; right of Malachi is all about grace.

When divided this way, why would anyone ever want to read the Old Testament? We all would prefer grace rather than law, so why not just focus exclusively on the good news of the New Testament?

Sadly this is the slippery slope many believers are on today without truly seeing God's Word in its entirety or from a clear perspective. When we view the God of the Tanakh (Old Testament) as mean and judgmental, we will naturally lean more on the grace-filled truths of the B'rit Hadashah (New Testament). Yet when we do this, we unconsciously begin to give the Old Testament less weight than the New Testament. As the Old Testament's value decreases in our eyes, we spend less time in it and begin to think of it as far less relevant. And the more we do this, the more our perspective of God changes. We distort His supposed Old Testament facets—His holiness, justice, or wrath, for example—and opt to focus on His more desirable traits that do not challenge us as much. Eventually we begin to believe—first subconsciously and then more overtly—that part of the Bible (the "really Jewish part") does not apply to us anymore, that it is irrelevant. We become New Testament believers who "live under the new covenant, and not the old," and to us that means we can ignore all the old stuff.

This is not a new problem. Jesus apparently noticed people sliding on the same slippery slope and confronted the issue head-on in His most famous teaching, the Sermon on the Mount, found in Matthew 5–7.

NOT TO ABOLISH, BUT TO FULFILL

Jesus' message to those tempted to diminish the Old Testament's value begins in Matthew 5:17, a verse I quoted earlier and one we will refer to often throughout this book: "Do not think that I have come to abolish the Law or the Prophets. I have not come to abolish, but to fulfill." With thousands of Jews hanging on His every word, Jesus immediately established a fundamental truth that we must not miss: the Old Testament *really* matters! Everything Jesus did on earth was in accordance with the laws God gave Moses in the Torah. This was the standard of living for God's chosen people, to keep them distinct from all other nations and marked as consecrated for God. Because the Jews of Jesus' day still believed they were indeed God's covenant people, they still acknowledged this Law to be God's requirement for them.

Notice, however, that Jesus did not just highlight the Torah (the Law) and leave out the rest of the Tanakh. By specifically referring to "the Law or the Prophets," He was pointing to the entire Tanakh—all three parts. In fact, in Luke 24:44 Jesus specifically mentioned all three when He said, "These are the words which I spoke to you while I was still with you, that all things must be fulfilled which were written in the Law of Moses and in the Prophets and in the Psalms concerning Me."

By rejecting the notion that He intended to do away with God's requirements (the Law) and His promises (the Prophecies), Jesus both submitted Himself to these standards and elevated the importance of the entire Old Testament. We must remember there was no New Testament in Jesus' time; His Bible *was* the Hebrew Bible, the Tanakh. And yet what He said in the next few verses of Matthew 5 directly addresses those who, in the generations to come, would argue that the Tanakh is less important or even irrelevant. When speaking of the Old Testament, Jesus said:

> For truly I say to you, until heaven and earth pass away, not one dot or one mark will pass from the law until all be fulfilled. Whoever, therefore, breaks one of the least of these commandments and teaches others to do likewise shall be called the least in the kingdom of heaven. But whoever does and teaches them shall be called great in the kingdom of heaven. For I say to you that unless your righteousness

> exceeds the righteousness of the scribes and Pharisees, you
> will in no way enter the kingdom of heaven.
>
> —MATTHEW 5:18–20

Jesus not only held up the Old Testament and validated it by adhering to its standards but also fulfilled those standards. He did not break any of the Law's commandments, *and* He fulfilled every Messianic prophecy found in the Nevi'im (Prophets) and Ketuvim (writings such as Psalms and Proverbs). Incredible!

Of course, most Jewish people in Jesus' time did not believe He fulfilled everything in the Tanakh, and the vast majority of Jews have held this view ever since. But notice how Jesus, immediately after legitimizing the Hebrew Bible, focused on the connection between understanding it and greatness in God's kingdom. According to Jesus, those who know how to use the Tanakh and who teach its commandments will be called great in God's kingdom. And those who disregard the Hebrew Bible and lead people astray regarding the Law will be considered the least in God's kingdom. Simply put, Jesus really valued the Old Testament and said we should too!

Later in Matthew's account Jesus conveyed this message from a different angle by using different word pictures around the central theme of finding a hidden treasure. At that point in His ministry Jesus had begun to use parables to teach the crowds about His Father's kingdom. Even His own disciples were confused by these analogies loaded with meaning, yet Jesus affirmed them by saying, "It is given to you to know the mysteries of the kingdom of heaven" (Matt. 13:11). Stated another way, they were to search fervently to find God's truth in His words, just as a man would sell everything he owned to buy a field with treasure in it (v. 44) or a merchant would sell all he had for a single pearl he has discovered (vv. 45–46). (In case you were wondering, we are to do the same.)

When the disciples finally began to understand His message, Jesus gave them yet another analogy to make a crucial point: "Therefore every teacher of the law who has become a disciple in the kingdom of heaven is like the owner of a house who brings out of his

storeroom new treasures as well as old" (Matt. 13:52, NIV). What law
was Jesus referring to? The Law of Moses—the Torah! In fact, I like
how accurately the Tree of Life Version of the Bible, translated by
Jewish believers, puts it: "Therefore every *Torah* scholar discipled for
the kingdom of heaven is like the master of a household who brings
out of his treasure both new things and old" (TLV).

We who value the Torah, and indeed the whole Hebrew Bible,
will find ancient treasures awaiting us the more we dig into it. The
Hebrew Bible may be buried for some people, but it is not lost or
forgotten. The more we search God's Word in its entirety, the more
we discover the riches waiting to be found in both the old (Hebrew
Bible) and the new (New Testament).

A NEW COMMANDMENT

Hebrews 4:12 compares the Word of God to a double-edged sword,
and I believe there are likewise two sharp sides to valuing the Hebrew Bible. If we go too far with either approach, taking things to
the extreme, we can cause spiritual injury. One extreme is what we
have already mentioned: living without any consideration of the
Tanakh. When we neglect the value of the Hebrew Bible and think
it matters little because we are "New Covenant believers," we do exactly what Jesus warned us of in Matthew 5 and are called the "least"
in His kingdom (v. 19). Clearly it is to our advantage to mine for the
treasures found in the Tanakh.

Yet on the other extreme is something I have also observed among
Christians who go overboard in rediscovering the Jewish roots of
their faith. In their zeal for honoring the Torah, they eventually return to living under the burden of the law. They become so obsessed
with following "the smallest letter" of the law that they lose sight of
Jesus, who fulfilled the law in their place.

Jesus broke down all the legalism by summing up the entire law—
including all the details of eating kosher and not breaking Shabbat
and not being defiled—in a single command: "Everything you would
like men to do to you, do also to them, *for this is the Law and the*

Prophets" (Matt. 7:12, emphasis added). Not long after, He defined this as a "new commandment" to His disciples, even though it had been the underlying theme of the Mosaic Law all along. "A new commandment I give to you," He said, "that you love one another, even as I have loved you, that you also love one another" (John 13:34). In fact, by following this new law of love, we would be marked as followers of the One who fulfills the law: "By this all men will know that you are My disciples, if you have love for one another" (v. 35).

Paul echoed the same new law in his letter to the Romans:

> He who loves another has fulfilled the law. For the commandments, "You shall not commit adultery, You shall not murder, You shall not steal, You shall not give false testimony, You shall not covet," and if there are any other commandments, are summed up in this saying, "You shall love your neighbor as yourself." Love works no evil to a neighbor. Therefore love is the fulfillment of the law.
>
> —Romans 13:8–10

Love is the fulfillment of the law. We know that God is love (1 John 4:7) and that He put this love on earthly display in the form of Jesus, who then "laid down His life for us" (1 John 3:16; see also John 3:16). So therefore *Jesus* is the fulfillment of the law.

That is ultimately the heart of this book. My goal is to show how Jesus fulfills everything in the Law and the Prophets and, in doing so, is the completion of Judaism itself. But before we can delve into how Jesus fulfills Judaism, which is the solution, we must first address the problem. If Jesus did not come to abolish the law but to fulfill it (Matt. 5:17), why, then, are Judaism and Christianity, in fact, two separate movements? If Jesus is the unifying element, the common denominator, and the fulfillment for both Jews and Christians, why have they become so separated?

To begin answering these questions, let's first examine one of the core elements of Jesus as the fulfillment of both—namely His Jewishness.

CHAPTER 2

THE JEWISHNESS OF JESUS

CAN YOU IMAGINE being in a Bible study with Jesus during His time on earth? I have heard many gifted Bible teachers in my life, but not one could come even remotely close to topping Jesus as a teacher of the Word. He *is* the Word, after all!

Now imagine having Jesus as your Bible study teacher not just for learning about a single passage, chapter, or book of the Bible, but instead for all of Scripture. This was the case for two fortunate men on a seven-mile walk from Jerusalem to a town called Emmaus. The Bible reveals very little about these men; in fact, only one of them is named at all. We know Cleopas (the man specifically mentioned) was a disciple of Jesus and that he and a fellow disciple were leaving Jerusalem and traveling to Emmaus after a whirlwind of events that had their heads spinning. Jesus, their rabbi, had been arrested during the night by Jewish authorities, crucified the next morning by Roman officials as though He were a murderer, and hurriedly buried in a nearby tomb. Everything had happened so quickly and unexpectedly that Cleopas and the other disciples were all left in a daze.

These two men had no idea that Jesus had risen from the dead. They were unaware His tomb was empty. So it is completely understandable why they would never have expected Jesus to join them on their journey. He was supposed to be dead, after all! And yet even when Jesus walked alongside them, they did not know it was Him. Their heads were so foggy from confusion and distraught, and Yeshua was temporarily disguised; Scripture says "their eyes were kept from recognizing Him" (Luke 24:16).

Luke 24:13–35 gives the amazing account of Jesus joining these two men on the road to Emmaus, but let me take some creative license in retelling the scene. Again, it began when neither disciple recognized his rabbi as He sauntered alongside them and essentially said, "Hey guys, whatcha talking about?"

"You've gotta be kidding me!" Cleopas answered peevishly, maybe from a lack of sleep. "I know you're an out-of-towner and all, but seriously, have you had your head in the sand these days, or what?" (I imagine he later regretted saying that.)

Cleopas and the other disciple then began to unpack all the events that had transpired over the previous four days, informing the very one who had been the centerpiece of it all. Although Jesus played dumb at first, it did not take long for Him to unload. After a quick rebuke for their lack of discernment—"You guys still don't get it?!"— He uncoiled the red thread running throughout God's Word to reveal Himself. More precisely, Luke says, "Beginning with Moses and all the Prophets, He explained to them the things concerning Himself in all the Scriptures" (Luke 24:27). "Beginning with Moses" means He started at the Tanakh's very first book, B'resheet (Genesis), just as we would.

I imagine Jesus started with, "In the beginning God created…" and then paused mid-sentence to ponder how ironic it was that He— the One who created the concept of time and "the beginning" itself— was now having to explain divine history as He stood on the very dust from which He formed these two men's forefather, Adam.

Jesus worked His way through each book of the Torah and then moved on to the Nevi'im (the prophetic books) and through the Ketuvim (the poetic and historical books and others such as Ecclesiastes, Lamentations, and Esther). I have no idea how Jesus walked them through every single scripture that related to Him in a mere hour and a half, considering that some scholars list as many as four hundred–plus Messianic prophecies in the Tanakh.[1] But by the same token, I do not know how it was possible for these two men to not recognize their rabbi after Jesus appeared to them, talked to them, walked beside them, and hung out with them for so long. Consider the fact that these were no casual followers of Jesus. Disciples in that day literally mimicked whatever their rabbi did, meaning they, out of all people, would have been able to spot Jesus in a crowd, much less on a relatively empty dirt road to Emmaus.

If Jesus, in His resurrected body, could walk through walls and teleport to locations far away, then I have to believe He was also fully capable of offering the most thorough revelation of Scripture in record time. I do not know how it was done, just as I do not know what Jesus said; I just know what Scripture says and that He changed their lives after this encounter, as He always does.

The world would be a different place if that Bible study could have been recorded. Sidewalk evangelists and jungle missionaries could save their own pleas and simply replay Jesus' amazing overview of Scripture concerning Him. For Cleopas and his companion, the imprint of this unforgettable revelation stirred them like nothing else could. "Did not our hearts burn within us while He talked to us on the way and while He opened the Scriptures to us?" they said emphatically after He suddenly vanished (Luke 24:32). Though Luke adds that "their eyes were opened, and they recognized Him" (v. 31), their case of temporary spiritual blindness is not uncommon. Most Jews throughout history have had the same condition, unable to see Yeshua (Jesus) as HaMashiach ("the Messiah"). Likewise, more than two-thirds of the world's population today cannot see Jesus— either by choice or because no one has revealed Him to them.[2] Only Jesus knows the actual number of those who truly follow Him today and those who do not. Paul says, "The god of this world has blinded the minds of those who do not believe," and we know that Satan is still responsible for many being unable to see the Light of the world (2 Cor. 4:4).

What I find fascinating, however, is the extent to which Satan has also succeeded in clouding believers' vision of who Jesus actually was while on earth and who He continues to be in heaven. I am not speaking here of Jews, Muslims, atheists, or any other groups generally blinded in their ability to see Jesus for who He really is. No, I am referring to those who claim to follow Jesus—Christians—but who do not recognize the importance of this simple fact: Jesus was a Jew. Indeed, among Christians today, there is a seriously debilitating shortsightedness of the Jewish Jesus, and it continues to take a toll on the church.

INTENTIONALLY JEWISH ROOTS

Jesus was a Jew.

That should not come as a shock, and yet it is astounding how many believers disregard this fundamental fact and trade it in for a "Christianized" version of Jesus. I will discuss in a later chapter how and why Christianity sterilized the Jewishness of Jesus, but for now it is more important to understand this truth: Jesus never came to establish a religion. Christianity as a religion was not His goal. You cannot find Him mentioning plans of starting a global religious establishment that would one day include 2.2 billion constituents and fragment into a zillion different denominations, organizations, and groups.[3] The truth is, the word Christianity is not even in the Bible. Though the word Christian is in the Bible, it is only used three times. (See Acts 11:26, 26:28, and 1 Peter 4:16.)

In its purest form, the term Christian describes a person who follows the Christ. The word Christ is the Greek translation of the original Hebrew word Mashiach, which means "anointed one." So a Christian is simply one who follows the anointed one. And who is the anointed one? Jesus, the Messiah.

If Christian was used to describe followers of Jesus even when the New Testament was being written, then why isn't the word Christianity also in the Bible? Because Christianity was a term that arose after the time of Jesus—even after the New Testament was written—to define the movement of followers who believed in Him. The Book of Acts records the details of this movement's early days, yet not once do we find this called Christianity or even described as a religion. The emergence of such an institutional organization would not happen until generations later (which we will track throughout the first part of this book).

Jesus never came to start something separate from what God had already established in the Hebrew Scriptures. His mission on earth was not to launch a new religion called Christianity but to complete and fulfill the revelation first given to the Jewish people. This is why Jesus never used the terms Christian or Christianity. It was not just an element of historical timing; it was because He was a Jew! He was HaMashiach—the Messiah, the Anointed One sent to save and redeem the Jewish people, just as the prophets foretold. In Matthew 15:24 Jesus declared, "I was sent only to the lost sheep of the house of Israel." This did not mean that Jesus' plan was not to save all but simply that His mission had to begin—as previous prophets' missions had begun—with Israel. Similarly Paul, upon entering a city where Jews lived, would always begin his ministry in that city by going first to the synagogue. He told the Romans that the power of God for salvation was "first to the Jew, then to the Gentile" (Rom. 1:16, NIV).

So Jesus came specifically to complete the purpose for the Jewish people and to fulfill the Scripture God had given them—all of which pointed to Himself. Although He was the Son of God, existing far above any religious boxes or labels, He came to a specific, chosen people as one of their kind. Jesus is called "Son of David" at least fifteen times in the Gospels, and this reiterates His completely Jewish roots.

What is fascinating to consider is that Jesus *chose* to be Jewish. He is the only naturally born Jew in history who chose His Jewishness. He made this decision in heaven with full intentionality, laying aside His deity in humility to become a man—a Jewish man—so that He would fulfill God's plan for salvation to come from the Jews first (John 4:22). If Jesus chose this way, then how can we disregard His choice by neutering His Jewishness to make Him fit a more religious "Christian" mold? Sadly this is what the Christian church has done throughout history.

JUST HOW JEWISH WAS JESUS?

To understand why Jesus chose to do everything through the Jewish context, let's take a closer look at the extent of His Jewishness.

Jesus was born into Jewish royalty.

Jesus was, simply put, a Jew's Jew. His lineage proved there was no doubt whatsoever of His Jewishness, and Matthew establishes this in the very first verse of his Gospel by calling Christ "the Son of David, the son of Abraham" (1:1). Not only is Jesus genetically linked to the original Jewish covenant through Abraham, but He is also linked by blood to the house of Israel's kings, from which the Messiah had to come. Being born into the tribe of Judah, in the house of David, was genetic gold, and yet isn't it interesting how fervently the priests and religious leaders of Jesus' day opposed Him for power once He began to talk of another kingdom?

Jesus was born King of the Jews.

This was not just declared over Him with a sign upon the cross. Jesus was correctly recognized as the King of the Jews even as a baby. "Now after Jesus was born in Bethlehem of Judea in the days of Herod the king, wise men came from the east to Jerusalem, saying, 'Where is He who was born King of the Jews? For we have seen His star in the east and have come to worship Him'" (Matt. 2:1–2). How wise these men truly were!

Jesus was circumcised on the eighth day.

Luke 2:21 records the normal procedure for any Jewish boy, physically marking Him as part of God's covenant people.

Jesus was dedicated in the temple.

After Joseph and Mary had Jesus circumcised, they took their firstborn to the temple in Jerusalem to have Him presented, or dedicated, to the Lord, according to the Mosaic Law that every firstborn child is to be set aside to God (Luke 2:22–23).

Jesus was raised by practicing Jewish parents.

Luke 2 gives us even more insight into just how Law-abiding Joseph and Mary were. As observant Jews, they made a trip to the temple forty days after Jesus' birth to make sacrifices as part of Mary's purification rituals after giving birth (vv. 22–24). They then offered a pair of doves or pigeons in obedience to the Torah's instructions.

Jesus celebrated Passover every year.

Jesus' parents established a standard during His childhood by making an annual pilgrimage to the Holy City for Passover (Luke 2:41). Based on the other indications we have of Joseph's and Mary's adherence to the Jewish Law, it is likely they made many other trips to Jerusalem, as Passover was one of three feasts that had to be observed in Jerusalem. This means Jesus probably grew up accustomed to visiting His Father's house, the temple.

Jesus read and studied a Hebrew Bible.

All Jewish children grew up learning from the Tanakh, as Deuteronomy 6:7 (part of the Shema) commanded parents to teach the Lord's ways "diligently" to their children and "talk of them" (His ways) throughout everyday life. Given Joseph's and Mary's faithfulness to follow the rest of the Law, Jesus likely spent significant time as a young boy under Joseph's tutelage, hearing and discussing the Hebrew Bible. But Jesus probably did this outside His home as well. At age five most Jewish boys began attending school at the local synagogue, where six days a week their studies—reading, writing, arithmetic, and other subjects—all centered on the Torah. Here Jesus would have memorized entire chapters from Moses' writings under the guidance of a rabbi.[4]

Although the Gospels do not focus much on Jesus' childhood, it is interesting that Luke specifically mentions how Christ at an early age "grew and became strong in spirit, filled with wisdom" (2:40). This was before Luke's account of a twelve-year-old Jesus getting left by His parents in the temple, which means even as a youngster He gained remarkable wisdom in His Father's ways by studying the Hebrew Bible. It is no wonder, then, that He hung around the temple teachers, "listening to them and asking them questions. All who heard Him were astonished at His understanding and His answers" (vv. 46–47).

As He grew older, Jesus would have moved on to study and memorize the Nevi'im and Ketuvim, as was the typical educational progression for Jewish adolescents.[5] By the time He was a young man, He knew entire books of the Hebrew Bible from heart and could discuss interpretations of the Tanakh with rabbis and adults alike. Still, Luke's comments—along with other scriptures—hint that even among a people well versed in the Scriptures and a Jewish culture that used the Tanakh as its textbook for every school subject, Jesus stood out for His exceptional knowledge of the Hebrew Bible.

Finally, at the start of His ministry we see that Jesus related to the Tanakh not only as a teaching document—quoting from it as a teaching tool ("It is written…")—but also as a weapon against the enemy. When Satan tempted Jesus at His weakest point, the Lord stood strong against his attacks by using Jewish Scripture that had been ingrained in Him since an early age. (See Matthew 4:1–11.)

Jesus was recognized as a Jewish rabbi.

We know Jesus followed in His earthly father, Joseph's footsteps by training and working as a carpenter (Matt. 13:55; Mark 6:3). But Jesus was obviously so remarkable in His understanding of the Hebrew Bible that He earned the respectful title of *rabbi*—teacher, master, great one—by people in all social spheres (Matt. 19:16; 22:35–36; Luke 12:13). Think about it: Do you really think the Pharisees and Sadducees, who closely protected their elite status as "guardians of the Law," would call Jesus *rabbi* if He had not already proved that He knew the Tanakh inside and out? John 3:1–2 shows that Nicodemus, a Pharisee "ruler of the Jews," addressed Jesus saying, "Rabbi, we know that You are a teacher who has come from God. For no one can do these signs that You do unless God is with him."

Jesus chose twelve Jews to be His disciples.

The dozen men Jesus chose to invest in may have been from completely different walks of life, but those walks were all within Jewish society. Entire books could be written about why Jesus handpicked these men rather than others. But the fact that He chose only Jews already tells us just how targeted His ministry was to the descendants of Abraham. Besides, can you imagine the complications that would have arisen on a daily basis if there had been a Gentile or two among the Twelve? Within any other culture such mixture possibly could have worked, but in the Jewish context—where everything Gentile was considered unclean—it was virtually impossible. This shows how deeply committed God was to salvation being to the Jew first (Rom. 1:16).

Jesus ministered mostly to Jews.

It is easy for us today to see how Jesus' main mission and ministry on earth extended far past the Jewish people. If you are a Gentile, you are a product of that extension, having been "grafted" into the Jewish covenant with God (Rom. 11:17–24). But we also must not forget that saving Gentiles was not Jesus' initial focus, which is why He spent the overwhelming majority of His time ministering to Jews. Granted, the Gospels record instances where Jesus broke with Jewish tradition and did the unthinkable by touching, healing, teaching, and loving on "unclean" Gentiles. Some of His biggest miracles occurred in Gentile territory. (See Matthew 15:30–38.) And yes, some of Jesus' teachings blatantly foretold that Gentiles would benefit from the salvation He offered.

But if you listed the amount of time Jesus spent among Jewish people compared with Gentiles, it would quickly become evident whom Jesus' target audience was. Jesus bluntly stated to a Canaanite (Gentile) woman, "I was sent only to the lost sheep of the house of Israel" (Matt. 15:24). During one point in His ministry He reminded His disciples to not seek out ministering to Gentiles but to "go rather to the lost sheep of the house of Israel" (10:6). Clearly Jesus' first focus was on reaching His own people, the Jews.

Jesus was crucified on Passover as "The King of the Jews."

The wise men were truly wise in declaring baby Jesus as the everlasting King of His people. Years later, however, Pontius Pilate was a mere puppet in an unfolding prophetic tidal wave surrounding Jesus' crucifixion. I doubt the Roman prefect knew the true significance of his words when he insisted on posting a sign that heralded Jesus as "The King of the Jews" (John 19:19–22). Was he intentionally mocking Jesus or just trying to further agitate the Jewish people who ingratiatingly claimed to "have no king but Caesar" (v. 15)? The answer is up for interpretation. But what we do know is that the entire ordeal surrounding Jesus' arrest, trial, sentencing, and crucifixion was, at its core, a *Jewish* matter taking place on Passover. Even with Roman government involved, the question still was whether Jesus was indeed who He claimed to be: the King of the Jews.

Jesus sent the Holy Spirit on the Jewish feast Shavuot.

It is no coincidence that the Lord fulfilled His promise of sending the Holy Spirit on a deeply significant Jewish holiday. Most Christians think of the Holy Spirit's outpouring in Acts 2 as a "Christian" event that birthed the church in fire and power. Yet hundreds of years before this, the Jewish people celebrated Shavuot (Pentecost is the Greek term) to mark a different yet equally significant arrival—that of the Torah. Shavuot falls on the fiftieth day after Passover and was set aside as a day of rest to remember God giving the Torah. It also commemorates the firstfruits of the harvest, as commanded in Leviticus 23:15–16, 21.

We do not know exactly how long the early believers gathered together to wait for the Holy Spirit's arrival; we know only that He came fifty days after Passover—which means they would have been celebrating Shavuot. It is possible they were gathered at a home eating the traditional holiday dairy meal, giving thanks to God for giving the Torah hundreds of years earlier and praying for His timing on giving the gift of the Holy Spirit. But undoubtedly Jesus knew the significance of that day and the power that would mark it in both the Word and now the Spirit as well.

Jewish tradition teaches that it was on this day of Shavuot, or Pentecost, when God appeared to His people on top of Mount Sinai and spoke to them so that they heard His voice. It is amazing to me that on this same day fifteen hundred years later God once again appeared in fire as He had on Mount Sinai and that He again spoke to His people by His Spirit, whom they no longer saw on top of a mountain but instead experienced within them.

Jesus sits in heaven as the Lion of Judah.

Although it is difficult to ignore Scripture's clear depiction of Jesus as a Jew while He lived on earth, some might argue that this was just a temporary circumstance for God's Son and that His Jewishness therefore matters little in the long run. Yet the Bible itself proves how much Jesus' Jewishness still matters, and one of the most convincing evidences of this is found in Revelation 5. During John's incredible vision of the worship surrounding God's throne, the apostle weeps when he discovers no one can open the scroll held in God's right hand, which will usher in a new glorious era for the world. But before John's grief escalates, an elder sitting around the throne tells him, "Do not weep. Look! The Lion of the tribe of Judah, the Root of David, has triumphed. He is able to open the scroll and to loose its seven seals" (v. 5).

Isn't it interesting that even in heaven, countless generations after He physically walked upon earth, Jesus is still referred to in connection with one of Israel's tribes? This is because Jesus has no plans of shedding His Hebrew identity. He is just as Jewish in heaven as He was on earth! This is significant, as it proves Jesus will always be the living fulfillment of every scripture related to Him.

In the very first book of the Bible, Genesis, we find a prophetic reference to Jesus as the Lion of Judah. Genesis 49:9-10 says, "You are a lion's cub, Judah; you return from the prey, my son. Like a lion he crouches and lies down, like a lioness—who dares to rouse him? The scepter will not depart from Judah, nor the ruler's staff from between his feet, until he to whom it belongs shall come and the obedience of the nations shall be his" (NIV). And in the very last book of the Bible, Revelation, we find the same reference to Jesus as the Lion of Judah. Out of all the titles given to Jesus in Scripture's Messianic prophecies, I find it fascinating that this one continues in heaven, as recorded by John. Jesus was Jewish, and He will forever be Jewish.

Jesus is coming back as the Root and Offspring of David.

Jesus is called the Lion of Judah in heaven, yet there is also one title He gives Himself that again shows His continuing Jewishness. In fact, this self-description is found in His last words recorded in the Bible. Jesus says in Revelation 22:16, "I am the Root and the Offspring of David, the Bright and Morning Star."

Not only does Jesus describe Himself by associating with David, Israel's greatest king, but His description indicates something profound that can only be possible through Him. Jesus is both the root (the beginning) and the offspring (the fruit). If you think about it, this is logically impossible. Nothing can be both the creator and the created...except for Jesus! He was the root of all peoples but describes Himself in particular as the root of Israel's royal line—through David. And He is the offspring of David biologically, as we have already seen in Jesus' lineage recorded in Matthew. The same person who created the Jewish line lives today as its ultimate fulfillment!

LOSING HIS RELIGION

As we can see, Jesus was born as a Jew, lived as a Jew, died as a Jew, and continues to reign in heaven today as a Jew. It is foolish, then, to separate Yeshua HaMashiach from a Judaic context—and yet that is exactly what Christians have done for generations. While most Jews subconsciously prefer to disassociate Jesus from their race, Christians have neutered His Jewishness by highlighting those elements of His identity that are less divisive to Gentiles.

For example, it is much easier to think of Jesus as a rabbi when you strip away the Jewish elements of that word (which is Hebrew, by the way) and instead make Him a teacher or leader. Yet this is like calling a dog a German shepherd but then saying she has nothing to do—not even in her lineage—with Germany, sheep, or herding. It is impossible and foolish, and yet this is exactly what we often do with Jesus' Jewish identity.

Rabbi is a strictly Jewish term given to those who teach the ways of the Torah and other aspects of Jewish life. In a way, a rabbi is an expert in all things Jewish. How is it possible, then, that so many Christians see Jesus as merely someone who taught the ways of God and "just happened" to be living in a Jewish context—as if God spun a wheel of fortune in heaven and the Jewish people were the lucky, albeit random, winners of the "Jesus-Picks-a-Human-Race" lottery?

Yes, Jesus did not come to establish a religion. Because of this, He seemed to go out of His way to prove that His kingdom was greater than the man-made rules and regulations that had turned many Jewish people away from a relationship with God into following a religion. But even within that context—of both the Jewish people and Judaism—Jesus elected to not do away with the Law God had given His chosen people; instead, Yeshua pointed out that He was the fulfillment of that Law and of every other aspect of what it meant to be Jewish.

Christianity has overlooked this for centuries. As a result, Judaism is seen as a completely separate way of faith. Even though the average Christian might acknowledge that a Jew worships the same God as him, he is far less likely to be conscious of the fact that he actually worships the Jew's God. Stated plainly, God was called upon by Jews long before He was called upon by anyone else, particularly Christians.

That leaves us with a single question, then: How did this happen? What made these two streams of faith become so separate if they stem from one source? If Jesus did not come to start a new religion, then what happened? We know why Jews throughout history have tried to ostracize Jesus as a Jew, but why have Christians gone to a similar extreme by overlooking His Jewishness?

These are the questions we will attempt to answer in the next few chapters as we look at the factors involved in Judaism and Christianity separating.

PART I

WHY JUDAISM AND CHRISTIANITY SEPARATED

CHAPTER 3

JEALOUSY

L OVE MAY BE blind, but science can now prove it is jealousy that *makes* you blind—or at least distorts your vision. A few years ago researchers at the University of Delaware studied romantically involved couples who were separated by a curtain and told to observe images on different computers. The women were asked to distinguish specific landscape and architecture photos amid a barrage of other photos, which included both peaceful images of streams and also gruesome or graphic pictures. The men, meanwhile, were originally asked to rate the attractiveness of various landscape photos.

Then it got interesting. After a few minutes, the men received new instructions in front of their partners: they were now to rate the attractiveness of other single women shown to them.

Researchers discovered a clear drop in attentiveness among the women once their partners were told to look at other women. Not only were the female participants more distracted, but they also were less able to distinguish elements in pictures that before had seemed clear.[1] According to lead researcher Steven Most, jealousy truly can distort our vision. "When attention is preoccupied...we tend to miss things that appear right in front of our eyes," he said.[2]

Jesus could have made the same conclusion two thousand years earlier based on firsthand experience with His own people. He was the prophesied Messiah, sent by God to redeem Israel, as promised centuries before. Yet despite Jesus' performing countless miracles, repeatedly fulfilling those prophecies, and living a sinless life in front of the Jewish masses, many still could not see the truth of who He was, or they simply refused to believe it. In the case of the Jewish religious leaders, their jealousy was partly to blame for such distorted vision that caused them to miss the Messiah who "appeared right in front of their eyes."

What would cause such jealousy? They, out of all the Jewish people, knew the Tanakh best and should have been the first to recognize Jesus as the promised Messiah based on their understanding of Scripture and the evidence they witnessed firsthand. They wanted the Messiah to come. How, then, could they not believe He was the fulfillment of the Tanakh?

Jesus raised this issue in John 5 when He told them, "You search the Scriptures, because you think in them you have eternal life. These are they who bear witness of Me. Yet you are not willing to come to Me that you may have life" (vv. 39–40).

To begin to identify what caused Judaism and Christianity to separate, we must go back further in time than the early church and look at what caused Judaism to "separate" from accepting its own Messiah. If Jesus was the fulfillment of everything the Jewish people longed for—the hope of a nation restored to its God and its former glory—then what caused the religious leaders to hate Him so much and to stir the once-adoring crowds to turn on Him? I believe we find the tipping point immediately after Jesus raised His friend Lazarus from the dead.

THE MIRACLE THAT MADE THEM MAD

There is much we can mine from the amazing story involving Lazarus: how Jesus delayed His arrival so the miracle of raising someone from the dead would have greater impact upon those who might believe in Him; how Jesus met Lazarus' sisters, Martha and Mary, in such unique ways; the reasons why Jesus wept; why Jesus prayed aloud to the Father in front of those gathered around; and more. But to answer our original question and understand how it was possible for such educated men of the Tanakh to *not* recognize the Messiah walking before them, we must pay attention to the religious leaders' immediate response following Lazarus' resurrection.

Then the chief priests and the Pharisees assembled the Sanhedrin and said, "What shall we do? This Man is performing many signs. If we leave Him alone like this, everyone
will believe in Him, and the Romans will come and take
away both our temple and our nation."...So from that day
forward they planned to put Him to death.

—John 11:47–48, 53

Jesus' influence was surging at this point in His ministry. He was
already a superstar because word had spread throughout Judea, Sa-
maria, Galilee, and beyond of a rabbi who taught with unmatched
authority, fed thousands with virtually nothing, calmed storms and
walked on water, and healed countless physical disabilities. Indeed,
with this latest miracle the religious leaders—which included the
Pharisees, Sadducees, and temple chief priests, elders, and scribes—
realized Jesus would become a legend.

"If we leave Him alone like this, everyone will believe in Him..."

We do not know whether the leaders used the word *believe* to
mean people believing Jesus was the Messiah or just believing in
terms of following and supporting Him. But either way was a major
problem for Israel's leaders. If people were hanging on Jesus' every
word, then He could influence their thinking. And if He could influence their thinking, He could certainly influence their actions. He
could easily whip up His followers into a frenzy and lead an upris-
ing or revolt—after all, He had already talked about tearing down
the temple (John 2:19); what else might this "revolutionary" come up
with concerning both Jewish and Roman authorities? The religious
leaders knew that influence equals power, and anyone with the kind
of influence Jesus possessed posed a threat to their own.

Indeed, their power had been carefully orchestrated under Rome's
rule. Israel at that time was not a secular society but a religious one,
which meant its religious leaders were the gatekeepers of Jewish culture. Rome recognized this and knew the best way to maintain peace
and order among the Jewish people was to go through their religious
leaders. The temple leaders, Pharisees, and Sadducees were not just

empowered as religious leaders, then, but also as political leaders. As long as they were able to snuff out any potential political uprisings before they escalated, Israel could retain its customs and culture despite Roman occupation. Those customs and culture revolved around the temple, and therefore preserving their power—both religious and political—was of the utmost importance.

Jesus had performed major miracles before. But raising the dead? That reached a whole new level. Suddenly the authority of Israel's established leaders was threatened like never before. "If word gets out about this," they thought, "it could be the end of us." Behind their words lay a brewing jealousy of Jesus' true power. Their power was fragile and dependent entirely upon Rome; Jesus was showing supernatural power that had nothing to do with worldly government. Whether they wanted to admit it or not, God was behind Him. More and more people were beginning to believe that maybe, just maybe, this man was actually the Messiah.

"And the Romans will come and take away both our temple and our nation."

This statement sounds innocent enough at first glance, as if the religious leaders were true worshippers and true patriots. But their actions throughout the Gospels reveal the not-so-hidden agendas behind their words.* These men were among the wealthiest Jews who, more often than not, bribed and bought their way to power. For example, Rome blatantly selected the high priest according to the highest bidder, and since only a few priestly families had the kind of wealth to engage in such extortion, the succession of priests was kept within those families.[3]

The religious leaders were the buffer between Rome and the Jewish people, and with such an important position came many luxuries unavailable to other Jews. This was partly why they were concerned for Rome taking away "our nation." In their minds Jesus threatened

---

* It should be noted that not all of Israel's religious leaders were corrupt or opposed to Jesus. Scripture mentions a few honorable Pharisees—Nicodemus (John 3), Gamaliel (Acts 5:34), Paul (Phil. 3:5)—and we also know that some priests were among those joining the early church (Acts 6:7).

the current status quo with Rome, which, in turn, threatened their own status quo of wealth, luxury, and power.

What Fueled Their Jealousy

Jesus lambasted the Pharisees multiple times because of their hypocrisy; they claimed to be concerned about God's ways and His house, yet they used both for personal gain. Yeshua refused to play their political games and was committed to higher purposes than upholding Jewish customs; He wanted a repentant people committed to fearing God more than man. And this is why His words for the religious leaders were often so sharp. He was not out to gain their support but instead held up a standard of true godly righteousness rather than the man-made, religious kind.

The more Jesus proved His righteousness and authority—both with powerful words and supernatural actions such as raising Lazarus from the dead—the more the religious leaders despised Him. Their jealousy raged to such an extent that John already mentions their desire to kill Him by the fifth chapter of his Gospel account (5:16, 18). Jesus was intruding on their territory and was a threat to their power. Something needed to be done.

Think about it: Jesus' actions in no way warranted an emotional response that involved murder. At this point, Jesus had done nothing deserving of being killed. Yes, He had surely upset the religious leaders after cleansing the temple early in His ministry. But their zeal for keeping the Law quickly spun out of control when after Jesus healed a lame man on Shabbat, they immediately "persecuted Jesus and sought to kill Him" (John 5:16). No rational person would desire to murder someone merely after an act of life-giving compassion on the "wrong" day. John adds another reason to their hatred: "So the Jews sought even more to kill Him, because He not only had broken the Sabbath but also said that God was His Father, making Himself equal with God" (v. 18).

In the next chapter we will look further into why Jesus' claim of God being His father was so offensive to the Jewish leaders. As

verse 18 shows, this claim had theological ramifications; if God was
Jesus' father, then it meant God had a son, which therefore meant
God was divided. This was blasphemy for any Jewish religious leader,
and under Jewish law blasphemy warranted death. These leaders saw
themselves as defenders of the Law and defenders of God Himself.
Their response to Jesus stemmed from a pride that elevated themselves to an elite spiritual status. God needed them, they thought,
and were it not for their righteousness through following the Law,
the people would not know either God or His Law. At the core Jesus
exposed their spiritual arrogance.

Already, then, we can see how the Jewish leaders' hatred of Jesus
was fueled by jealousy. On the surface their hostility toward Jesus
was about His breaking the Sabbath by healing a blind man on it as
well as His speaking about God being His father. And yes, He made
them mad by exposing their hypocrisy. Yet at the core of all these
issues was a jealousy over Jesus' supernatural power, His influence
with the masses, and His righteous authority. Mark 15:10 proves this
when it states plainly, "Pilate knew that the chief priests had brought
Jesus to him because they were jealous" (CEV).

Isn't it interesting that the seeds of separation between Judaism
and Christianity can be traced back to these moments of jealousy?
If we look at it from a broader perspective, we can see the beginning
of the fragmentation between faith in Jesus and the religion of the
traditional Jews of Jesus' time—which became the foundation of
modern-day Judaism—was rooted in the Pharisees' jealousy and fear
of Jesus. What began with Jesus healing a blind man on the Sabbath quickly bubbled over into an ongoing plot to murder Him that
reached its tipping point after Lazarus' resurrection.

The religious leaders envied His authentic power, as is evident
in Matthew 27:17–18: "So when they had gathered together, Pilate
said to them, 'Whom do you want me to release to you—Barabbas,
or Jesus who is called Christ?' For he knew that they had handed
Him over out of envy." They were jealous of His growing influence, which took away from their own. And they were fearful that
He would disrupt or destroy the power system they had so carefully

built for personal gain. In a nutshell, Jesus embodied the collapse of their world.

THE JEWISH REVOLT

Israel's leaders feared that a religious Jesus, gaining influence for His spiritual revelations, would diminish their own religious power over the Jewish public. Likewise, these leaders feared that a political Jesus, with an increasing number of followers wanting to see Israel restored as an independent nation, would diminish their own political power granted to them by Roman officials. Both arenas—religious and political—centered on the temple. So they assumed that killing Jesus, and other revolutionaries like Him, would keep the temple standing under an increasingly violent Roman empire.

They were wrong.

Though the temple stood for more than a generation following Jesus' death, by AD 70 Rome had had enough. Uprisings and full-fledged battles covered the land in what history calls the Jewish Revolt. The first revolt began in AD 66 after Judea's tax-heavy Roman procurator, Gessius Florus, stole large amounts of silver from the temple to compensate for a low-revenue season. Protesting Jews in Jerusalem temporarily overthrew Roman forces in Jerusalem, and for a brief moment the Zealots (a political sect that sought the end of Roman occupation) and other anti-Roman revolutionary groups convinced much of the Jewish population that they could defeat their oppressors. This belief was bolstered when additional Roman troops sent from Syria were also defeated.[4]

Until this point, Roman Emperor Nero had never considered Judea and its neighboring Jewish territories worth much attention. Those sent to govern the districts were of the lowest class of civil officers and deemed unworthy to command Roman legions—such was the lowly view of Judea in the Empire's eyes. Yet when Jerusalem continued to be embroiled in battles with Roman troops throughout AD 67–68, Nero eventually sent the respected military commander Vespasian with sixty thousand soldiers to quash the Jewish rebellion.[5]

Vespasian did not disappoint the emperor. His troops stormed into Galilee and either killed or enslaved an estimated one hundred thousand Jews.[6] Next, he conquered much of Judea. When Nero committed suicide and Vespasian eventually became emperor in AD 69, Vespasian sent his son, Titus, to handle matters in Jerusalem.

Within the city's walls, however, the Jewish people were fighting among themselves. Any surviving Zealots throughout Israel streamed into Jerusalem, the last fortress of hope for Israel's sovereignty. The Zealots overthrew and killed any Jews in leadership who did not support their cause. They even burned food supplies that could have fed Jerusalem's population for years during a Roman siege, claiming that it forced those inactive in the struggle to engage. In fact, Jewish historians claim that the civil war within Jerusalem possibly did as much damage as the Roman attack from the outside.[7]

That attack came during the summer of AD 70 when Roman forces breached Jerusalem's fortified walls. Jewish historian Josephus describes the Roman soldiers as if they were demonically possessed with rage and bloodlust, such was the damage they caused while sweeping through the city. After ravaging houses and buildings, the troops came to the steps of the temple, where many Jews had fled for safety. Despite both Vespasian's and Titus' urgings to not destroy the temple, the soldiers did not hold back, and God's house was soon overcome with flames. As the holy structure burned, Roman troops grabbed whatever spoils they could, which would eventually be paraded through Rome's streets as symbols of victory.[8]

Jerusalem and the Jewish people were left decimated. More than one million Jews died from the revolt, and for those who survived— including the ninety-seven thousand captured as slaves—their way of life was left in shambles.[9] The temple was not just a religious structure for them; it was their identity. Remember, Jewish society was entirely religious during this time. The core of their identity as a people, then, revolved around three things: the temple, the sacrifices, and the priesthood. God had commanded them to worship Him with sacrifices. He had established holy days such as Yom Kippur, the Day of Atonement, in which incense was offered in the holy of holies and two goats (one of which would be set free) were offered to make amends for the people's sins.

Various sacrifices were made throughout the year: the mandatory sin offerings and trespass offerings, and the freewill offerings (burnt offerings, peace offerings, and grain offerings). Israel's entire religious system involved coming closer to God through the sacrifices of animals. And God had instructed them to only sacrifice in the temple He had specifically designed. If they could no longer sacrifice in the manner God required—in the temple—then how would they approach Him?

Likewise, each of the sacrifices God instructed the Jewish people to offer required priests to administer it. God had originally appointed those from the tribe of Levi to be priests, ministering before Him both in ceremonial offerings and with their sanctified lives. They were the ones who could go before Him on behalf of the Jewish people. But without a temple and without sacrifices, what need was there for any kind of priesthood?

It is doubtful the Roman soldiers understood just how much damage they inflicted upon the Jewish people when they demolished the temple. In a single day the three primary pillars of Jewish identity—the temple, sacrifices, and priesthood—crumbled, leaving behind a people in ruins and, once again, seemingly abandoned by God.

THE NEW JEW

With the temple in ruins, it was impossible for Jewish life to go back to the way it was before. The remaining religious leaders did their best to unite the Jews, but even among their own ranks they were decimated. For example, the Sadducees slowly disappeared altogether following the temple's destruction because their teachings were so closely connecting to the structure. The Zealots, though not a religious group per se, were nearly wiped out from the revolt.

A few Pharisees and rabbis survived, however, and in AD 90 they gathered for the sole purpose of restoring the Jewish identity. We now call this meeting the Council of Yavneh, named for the southern coastal town where they met. Yavneh was becoming a post-temple spiritual center in part because of Rabbi Yochanan ben Zakkai, who had managed to flee Jerusalem during the Roman siege but before the temple's fall. Much is debated about the Council of Yavneh (also called Jamnia)—whether it was a one-time session or a process over years, whether those gathered decided upon a Jewish canon of the Hebrew Bible, and even whether the Council even happened.

I do not claim to be a historian and will not attempt to argue for or against any of those issues. But what I do know, and what can be verified from many rabbinical texts, is that whatever transpired at Yavneh in AD 90 was hugely significant in creating a "new Judaism" for Jews during a post-temple era that has continued to this day. As Jewish scholars Peter Shirokov and Eli Lizorkin-Eyzenberg write:

> Whether the sages held a special council or if their discussions about the holy books were ongoing, the enduring significance of Jamnia [Yavneh] lies not in the closing of the Jewish canon, but in ensuring the cultural and religious survival of the Jewish people. Prior to 70 AD, Judaism was fragmented into various sects. The Jamnia [Yavneh] sages intentionally promoted an inclusive, pluralistic and non-sectarian Judaism. In light of new circumstances, they created a more flexible system of Torah interpretation that accounted for diversity and charted a new way to relate to God and his covenant with Israel. They shaped the possibility of new Jewish faith and life without sacrifices, priesthood and the centrality of the Jerusalem Temple.[10]

The discussions at Yavneh (or Jamnia) centered on the Jewish people's survival: How could they ensure that their way of life—their cultures, customs, traditions, and religion—would outlive them? In an era in which their system of sacrifices was no longer physically possible, what would the Jewish people do instead? In essence, the fundamental question was this: What did it mean to be Jewish now that the temple was gone?

The answer, according to ben Zakkai and others, was found in forming new liturgy and traditions. They constructed new practices and requirements—outside of the Torah—to supplement or even replace parts of the Law. These ranged from the seemingly obvious replacements—such as ram's blood being sprinkled on the altar that no longer existed—to entirely new commandments (e.g., waiting several hours between eating meat and consuming dairy). From these new standards emerged what we today refer to as Rabbinic Judaism. In essence, what was birthed at Yavneh was a new definition of what it meant to be Jewish.

BIRTHED IN A FAMILIAR SPIRIT

The Jews wanted desperately to regain their identity as a people. The Council of Yavneh was designed for this purpose and provided a different variation of the Jewish life, birthed out of an intent to hold the Jewish people together. Of course some familiar foundational elements were still there in following the Torah. But now there emerged new standards that were to become new customs and traditions and would eventually define what Judaism was. But who exactly were the ones giving these instructions? Who were these rabbis that would shape the Jewish people for generations to come?

This was a critical question, particularly for Jews who followed Yeshua HaMashiach, because amid the new standards was a decidedly anti-Jesus slant. Within the new Jewish culture these rabbis presented was a belief that Jesus of Nazareth, who had been killed only a generation prior, was someone to be ignored and forgotten—just a tragic blip on the Jewish timeline filled with overzealous rabbis claiming to be sent from God. Their view was not against Christianity, for the Christian religion had yet to take shape; it was purely against Jesus and anyone who dared follow Him.

When you discover who these men really were, this is not surprising. The religious leaders who gathered at Yavneh to reinvent Judaism were, in fact, the grandsons of the same religious leaders who rejected Jesus. Remember, the leaders of Jesus' day operated out of jealousy and out of a fear of losing their own power. This is why they wanted Jesus killed. They then passed on their anti-Jesus mind-set to their sons and grandsons, who led the "reinvention" of Judaism in AD 90 and who eventually became the founders of today's Orthodox Judaism. Each generation of Jews since then inherited an anti-Jesus mind-set and spirit that has been continually passed on to the following generation. So within today's Judaism we can trace a hostile attitude toward Jesus going all the way back to the Pharisees who plotted to kill Him.

This is why every Jew inherently thinks following Jesus is "un-Jewish." Since the time of Yavneh, we have been told that to be Jewish is to not believe in Jesus. We do not know why we shouldn't believe in Jesus. We do not know why we shouldn't investigate His life more or read the Scriptures—the Tanakh or the B'rit Hadashah (New Testament)—to see whether we should believe in Him. We just pick up in our homes and community that we should not believe in Jesus. Why? Because that is what we do as Jewish people. Simply put, Jews do not believe in Jesus.

I find it tragic that countless Jews fall into this trap, not knowing that one of the reasons they reject Jesus lies at the heart of this "new Judaism" formed almost two thousand years ago. The Pharisees and religious leaders of Jesus' time wanted Him dead because they were jealous of Him—of His divine power, of the authority in which He used the Tanakh, and of the influence and favor He had with so many. They refused to examine the Scriptures, which they claimed to know so well, with open eyes, minds, and hearts to find that Yeshua fulfilled every prophecy regarding HaMashiach, just not in the way they thought.

The Pharisees and religious leaders who lived during and after the temple's destruction inherited this same anti-Jesus heart and mind-set because they came from the same family line. Just as Israel's leaders felt threatened by Jesus while He was alive, the new leadership in AD 90 felt threatened by an emerging force of Jesus followers who claimed Jesus was still alive. They wanted any vestiges of His existence wiped from the collective Jewish memory. To that extent, they constructed a new Jewish identity that included a clear opposition to anything remotely associated with Jesus. They wanted it to seem impossible to be Jewish *and* believe in Jesus.

Fast-forward two millennia, and their plan has worked, for the most part. Today most Jews blindly accept that they should not believe in Jesus, and the reason is simply because that is just what Jewish people do—they do not believe in Jesus. Most have unknowingly inherited the same hard-heartedness and refusal to look into the Tanakh with an open heart. So to some degree, the Pharisees and rabbis of two thousand years ago have succeeded; Judaism—following the Jewish way of life—is now seen as incompatible with following Jesus.

There is a problem, though. I am living proof that the two *are* compatible. You can be a Jew and a Christian. They are not mutually exclusive. A Jew is someone who is born physically from the lineage of Abraham, Isaac, and Jacob. Being a Jew is not defined by one's belief but rather by one's bloodline. This is why God commanded the Jewish boys to be circumcised on the eighth day, marking them as part of the household of Israel. They did not believe anything at eight days old but were still considered part of Israel because they were a physical descendant of Abraham, Isaac, and Jacob.

Being a Christian, however, is not about your physical lineage but about what you choose to believe. In fact, we read in the Book of Acts that the mother church in Jerusalem was almost exclusively made up of Jews who were following the Christ, which, by definition, makes them Jewish Christians. Again, the word Christ is the Greek word meaning "anointed one." It is the equivalent of the Hebrew word Mashiach. Because God's purpose in sending Jesus was to reach not only Israel but the whole world, He gave us the New Testament in Greek rather than Hebrew because Greek was the most common language of the world. Jesus was sent for everyone. So when a person follows the Christ, who is Jesus the Anointed One, he becomes a Christian, regardless of whether he is Jew or Gentile.

Logically speaking, if Jesus is, in fact, the Christ, the Anointed One, the Mashiach and promised Messiah of Israel, then there is nothing more Jewish that a Jew can do than to follow Him. He is the ultimate Jew, the King of the Jews—which is why the sign that hung above His head on the cross read "THIS IS JESUS THE KING OF THE JEWS" (Matt. 27:37). Jesus is the fulfillment of Judaism in every way. We have already seen in the previous chapter how Jewish Jesus really was, so following Him does not in any way renounce one's Jewishness.

I believe this truth could free millions of Jews around the world. I believe if their spiritual eyes could be opened, they would discover the same truth I have: that Yeshua truly is HaMashiach, that He lives today as the Lion of Judah and the Son of David, and that our Jewish Lord has the ultimate definition of what it means to be Jewish—namely a follower of Him!

CHAPTER 4

THEOLOGICAL CRISIS

IT DOESN'T TAKE much these days to earn a reality TV show. But if anyone deserves to have his fifteen minutes of fame on the small screen, it is David Drew Howe. After all, he is a king.

The forty-five-year-old beer-bellied auto mechanic from Frederick, Maryland, certainly does not look the part of royalty. You are far more likely to find him hanging out with coworkers at the repair shop or vacationing with his family than ruling a kingdom. But Howe discovered through an online search that he was an heir to the throne of the Isle of Man, a small, independent colony between England and Ireland. In 2008 he filed an official notice in the *London Gazette* announcing his intent to claim the throne, and when that was not contested, he posted a press release, packed his bags, and eventually traveled with his family to become the king of Man— with a reality TV crew recording his every step, of course.[1]

The program, called *Suddenly Royal*, followed Howe, his wife, and his daughter as they attempted to win over local citizens and act more royal while under the watchful guidance of an etiquette coach and royal advisor. As cousin to the Queen of England (yes, you read that right!), Howe and his family were also invited to Prince William and Kate Middleton's royal wedding. It did not take long, however, for their made-for-TV adventure to hit an impasse as the family discovered it preferred "normal" blue-collar life in Maryland to a blue-blood reign three thousand miles away. So after a ten-year journey to ascend the throne, Howe abdicated it in 2017 via—true to form—his website.[2]

Some of *Suddenly Royal*'s funniest scenes involved Howe informing Isle of Man residents that he was their king—to which most either balked or laughed heartily. "That's a good joke," one man chuckled while sitting at a local bar with the American who looked and acted more like a tourist than a ruler.[3]

Indeed, someone showing up and suddenly announcing himself as king can seem like a joke. But for the Jewish people, Jesus' claims of royalty were no laughing matter. In all truthfulness, Jesus only stated He was King to Pilate while on trial, and even then it was indirectly. "Are You the King of the Jews?" Pilate asked, to which Jesus answered, "You truly say so" (Luke 23:3). Pilate took no issue with this and seemed to rub the idea in the Jewish leaders' faces when he insisted on posting a sign above Jesus' cross heralding Him as "The King of the Jews" (John 19:19).

Though this offended the Jewish people, Jesus' claim to kingship was not the core issue for them. No, what bothered them most was His indirect assertion that He was the Son of God. In fact, this disturbed them so much that they tried to kill Jesus as soon as they heard His declaration. John records the tense scene:

> The Feast of the Dedication was at Jerusalem, and it was winter. Jesus walked in the temple in Solomon's Porch. Then the Jews surrounded Him, saying, "How long will You keep us in suspense? If You are the Christ, tell us plainly."
>
> Jesus answered them, "I told you, and you did not believe. The works that I do in My Father's name bear witness of Me. But you do not believe, because you are not of My sheep, as I said to you. My sheep hear My voice, and I know them, and they follow Me. I give them eternal life. They shall never perish, nor shall anyone snatch them from My hand. My Father, who has given them to Me, is greater than all. No one is able to snatch them from My Father's hand. My Father and I are one."
>
> Again the Jews took up stones to stone Him. Jesus answered them, "I have shown you many good works from My Father. For which of those works do you stone Me?"
>
> The Jews answered Him, "We are not stoning You for a good work, but for blasphemy, and because You, being a Man, claim to be God."

Jesus answered them, "Is it not written in your law, 'I said, "You are gods"'? If He called them 'gods,' to whom the word of God came, and the Scripture cannot be broken, do you say of Him, whom the Father has sanctified and sent into the world, 'You blaspheme,' because I said, 'I am the Son of God'? If I am not doing the works of My Father, do not believe Me. But if I do them, though you do not believe Me, believe the works, that you may know and believe that the Father is in Me, and I in Him." Again they tried to seize Him, but He escaped from their hands.

—JOHN 10:22–39

The Jews who confronted Jesus sincerely believed they would be doing God a favor by stoning this man who claimed deity. They were proud to be guardians of the Law, and the religious spirit in them rose up as soon as Jesus began speaking about God on familiar terms. "Blasphemy!" they cried. Not only was the Nazarene referring to God as if He were His Father and saying that He was one with God, but the Jewish crowd believed Jesus was also defiling God's name and character by bringing Him down to such an earthly level. According to their laws, Jesus deserved to be killed for cheapening God's holy and righteous name.

It is easy for us to look at this situation purely as believers on this side of the cross and forget just how controversial Jesus' claims were. For hundreds of years, God had established His holiness as one of the fundamental attributes His people were to recognize. He was a holy God who would not tolerate sin. They were a sinful people who needed to be cleansed in order to come close to Him. At times the Lord had to remind Israel of this truth with powerful yet destructive acts. He struck Uzzah dead for touching the ark of His presence (2 Sam. 6:6–7). He killed Nadab and Abihu, the priestly sons of Aaron, for not following His sacrificial instructions and for approaching Him as if He were just another God (Lev. 10:1–3). On several other occasions God judged those who treated His holiness flippantly.

And yet here was a man—an everyday carpenter from Nazareth,

no less!—who seemed to be doing the exact same thing by claiming to have a special relationship with Yahweh. This man was not a priest, not even the son of a priest. No one had declared Him a prophet to the nation in the mold of Isaiah or Jeremiah. In the eyes of the Jewish people confronting Jesus, the only evidence Jesus had to support His claims of being anything special were some offensive teachings, some powerful supernatural healings, and *rumors* of a voice from heaven addressing onlookers during His baptism.

That evidence should have been enough. As we addressed in the last chapter, had the Jewish leaders actually examined the Messianic prophecies of the Tanakh with open hearts, they would have found all clues pointing to Jesus. If they had listened more closely to Jesus' teachings and seen His healings without bias, they could have discovered the truth. But what kept them from believing, in part, was a major theological issue that Jesus' claim raised for them: How could God have a son?

A DIVIDED GOD

The Jewish faith was the first in human history to believe in one God. Its monotheistic theology and its idea of an uncreated deity is what set it apart from all other religions and cultures. That is why the idea of a singular God is so central to the Jewish belief system. Even in my conservative Jewish upbringing in Ohio, where God was mentioned occasionally but not really talked about much, I still remember hearing the words of the Shema each time I was in the synagogue: "Sh'ma Yisra'el! Adonai Eloheinu, Adonai echad" (Hear, O Israel: The LORD is our God. The LORD is one! [Deut. 6:4]). The typical Jewish paradigm sees this as the ultimate proof—a definition from God Himself—that God is a singular God. The oneness of God—that He is One within Himself—is core to our view of Him.

It was the same for the Jewish leaders of Jesus' time, which is why His claim to be God's Son was so incredibly offensive. If God had a son, then it meant He was divided, and this went against everything they knew and believed. If God were both a father and a son,

then He was two people, not one. This blew apart their theological
paradigms. They were raised to be hypersensitive to worshipping
false gods, since that had been such a problem in Israel's history, and
therefore the implications of Jesus' statements raised red flags for all
who heard Him. Surely this man was preaching a false message and
needed to be silenced!

Jesus regularly hit the Jewish leaders' nerves by referring to God
as His Father. It should be noted, however, that although He did
this frequently, Jesus only referred to Himself as the Son of God
twice, and in both instances He did it indirectly and without using a
first-person pronoun. In John 5, Jesus said:

> Truly, truly I say to you, whoever hears My word and be-
> lieves in Him who sent Me has eternal life and shall not
> come into condemnation, but has passed from death into
> life. Truly, truly I say to you, the hour is coming, and is now
> here, when the dead will hear the voice of the Son of God,
> and those who hear will live....I can do nothing of Myself.
> As I hear, I judge. My judgment is just, because I seek not
> My own will, but the will of the Father who sent Me.
> —JOHN 5:24–25, 30

Later, in John 11:4, upon receiving word that Lazarus was sick,
Jesus said: "This sickness is not unto death, but for the glory of God,
that the Son of God may be glorified by it."

Notice that in both passages Jesus never blatantly said, "I am the
Son of God," but instead referred to Himself in third person. Jesus
often put the validity of a specific title given to Him back upon those
making the assessment. For example, when the woman at the well
made a statement about the Messiah coming, Jesus simply replied,
"I who speak to you am He" (John 4:25–26). When Pilate asked if
Jesus was King of the Jews, the Lord succinctly stated, "You truly
say so" (Luke 23:3). And after washing His disciples' feet, Jesus said,
"You call me Teacher and Lord. You speak accurately, for so I am"
(John 13:13).

It is important for us to recognize, then, that Jesus most certainly did not go around touting His deistic titles. He instead spoke out of the authority that came from a deep relationship with His Father. Because He *was* one with the Father, Jesus could therefore make reference to this oneness without having to frequently declare it. In addition, He knew that the longer it took for the Jewish leaders' blood to boil over His claims to divine sonship, the more time He had to fulfill His ministry purposes on earth.

ONENESS IN THE FATHER AND SON

If the Jewish leaders had received true revelation of God's Word rather than just ingesting it as religious instruction, maybe then they would have noticed the error of their own theology. They could not think of God as a father and God as a son, and yet the Tanakh includes at least three strong references to this.

The first one is found in Psalm 2, one of the most well-known Messianic psalms. Its verses depict an end-times showdown involving the unified kings of the earth who rally together "against the LORD and against His anointed" (v. 2), the latter of which clearly refers to the Messiah. Only a few verses later God addresses this Anointed One, saying, "You are My son; this day have I begotten you. Ask of Me, and I will give you the nations for your inheritance, and the ends of the earth for your possession" (vv. 7–8). The psalm then concludes with the Lord advising the world's kings and judges to "Kiss the son, lest He become angry" (v. 12). Clearly we find references in this Scripture passage to God as the Father giving authority—as well as nations and territories—to God the Son.

Another place we find this same Father-Son theme is in Psalm 110, which is also a Messianic psalm quoted several times in the New Testament. David, the psalm's author, begins with a statement that at first glance may sound confusing: "The LORD said to my lord, 'Sit at My right hand, until I make your enemies your footstool'" (v. 1). Even Jesus highlighted this verse as troublesome to the Pharisees' theology without a Father-Son context. (See Matthew 22:43–44.) His teaching helps us understand that the first Lord refers to God the

Father, while the second refers to the Messiah, God the Son. And again, we see the Son empowered by the Father not just as One who will "judge among the nations" (Ps. 110:6) but also as "a priest forever after the order of Melchizedek" (v. 4).

The Tanakh gives other references pointing to the relationship within God. Yet perhaps none offers such a visual account of how this Father-Son relationship will play out in the end times as in the Book of Daniel. There the prophet includes a last-days vision of an exchange "within" the timeless Creator God. Daniel calls God the "Ancient of Days," a term unique to his book but powerful in its description of the Lord's eternality. In the vision the Ancient of Days sits on His fiery throne, with thousands upon thousands of creatures standing before Him. After alluding to what will happen to Satan and his evil forces, Daniel says:

> I saw in the night visions, and there was one like a Son of Man coming with the clouds of heaven. He came to the Ancient of Days and was presented before Him. There was given to Him dominion, and glory, and a kingdom, that all peoples, nations, and languages should serve Him. His dominion is an everlasting dominion, which shall not pass away, and His kingdom that which shall not be destroyed.
>
> —DANIEL 7:13–14

Can you see what is happening here? Daniel is watching an exchange between the Father and the Son! The Father is turning over the world to His Son, giving Him the kingdom that will never pass away or be destroyed. It is everlasting, just as He is. This is significant, for it means the Messiah Son of God, referred to here as "one like a Son of Man" is God Himself. (It is interesting to note that Jesus called Himself "Son of Man" more than any other title, just as He is referred to in this passage from Daniel.) The Father has given the Son all rights and authority to rule as God. This is why Jesus told His disciples, "All authority has been given to Me in heaven and on earth" (Matt. 28:18).

Jesus, as God the Son, only did the will of God the Father (John

5:19). Yeshua was such a mirror reflection of the Father that He could make statements such as "My Father and I are one," and "He who has seen Me has seen the Father," and "I am in the Father, and the Father is in Me" (John 10:30; 14:9, 11).

It is important to realize at least three distinctions Scripture makes regarding this unique relationship and what the Father has done through His Son, Jesus.

1) *The Father created the world through His Son.* The apostle John begins his book by describing Jesus, the Word, as existing "with God" from the beginning because He "was God. He was in the beginning with God. All things were created through Him, and without Him nothing was created that was created" (1:1–3). Jesus was not merely a bystander in heaven waiting until His time on earth. He *was* God, and Scripture even says, "For by Him all things were created that are in heaven and that are in earth, visible and invisible, whether they are thrones, or dominions, or principalities, or powers. All things were created by Him and for Him" (Col. 1:16).

2) *The Father saves people through His Son.* First John 4:14 states this truth as clearly and succinctly as possible: "And we have seen and testify that the Father sent the Son to be the Savior of the world." Likewise, the most famous verse in modern times conveys the same message: "For God so loved the world that He gave His only begotten Son, that whoever believes in Him should not perish, but have eternal life. For God did not send His Son into the world to condemn the world, but that the world through Him might be saved" (John 3:16–17). We know that God "does not want any to perish" and "desires all men to be saved" (2 Pet. 3:9; 1 Tim. 2:4), and He chose to bring salvation—both a

one-time saving and an ongoing *being* saved—through His Son, Yeshua HaMashiach.

3) *The Father will reign through His Son.* As we have already seen in the Messianic psalms and in Daniel's vision mentioned earlier, God the Father will at one point hand over the entire reign of this world to His Son, who will then rule in an eternal kingdom as its eternal King. Revelation 11:15 confirms this when it says, "The kingdoms of the world have become the kingdoms of our Lord, and of His Christ, and He shall reign forever and ever."

THREE IN ONE

During the early 1980s I attended Toccoa Falls College in the foothills of northeast Georgia. It was a solid Bible college, but my experience there proved that the school's leadership at that time was not open to the gifts of the Holy Spirit being used, and in particular the gift of tongues was not encouraged. This became most evident during one of my Bible classes when we dealt with the topic of how demons enter individuals. As part of the curriculum, we were required to listen to a tape series from an individual whose ministry focused on deliverance. This minister taught that many of the people whom he had delivered from demons actually received a demon when they tried to speak in tongues. This impacted me, and as a result of the school's atmosphere being non-Charismatic, particularly as it related to the gift of tongues, I was not interested in pursuing that gift.

There were, however, a few Charismatic students attending the college, and one of those was a friend of mine I'll call John. One evening my wife, Cynthia, and I were invited to have dinner over at John and his wife's home. After dinner, John and I got in a conversation about the gifts of the Holy Spirit, and he shared with me about the gift of tongues, which he had. As he was sharing with me, I felt a distinct witness from the Holy Spirit in my heart that my friend was speaking truth—that tongues was a real, authentic, good gift that the Holy Spirit could give.

While John was speaking, and as the Spirit was moving upon me, my friend suddenly stopped talking and asked me, "What are you feeling right now?" I am ashamed to say that I lied and replied, "Nothing."

Because what he was sharing with me was unfamiliar and because I had been taught that the gift of tongues was not something I should ask for, it was scary to me and not easy to receive. Praise God, I eventually came around. Although I do not believe that you have to speak in tongues to be Spirit-filled or that speaking in tongues makes you holier, I know what a precious gift it has been for me in my life. I thank God for His grace and patience with me.

Being confronted with unfamiliar things is not easy. It can feel scary, add a little stress, and maybe even cause full-fledged anxiety. When we do not fully understand something foreign that is presented as a truth we should accept, we can often feel threatened by it. I imagine this is exactly what the Jewish leaders experienced whenever Jesus spoke of His relationship with the Father God. His words were worse than nails on a chalkboard; they were entirely offensive to everything their Jewish faith stood for. They served a God who was one; Jesus' God sounded divided and, well, wrong.

Believe it or not, this is how many Jewish people today feel about Christians and the Trinity theology. Practicing Jews are raised with the Shema as the foundation of their religious belief system, while Christians (whether aware of it or not) inherently follow the Apostles' Creed, which depicts a triune God consisting of the Father, the Son, and the Holy Spirit. To most traditional Jews, this concept does not make sense. It sounds like three separate Gods, no matter how much Christians attempt to explain it otherwise.

This understanding—or lack thereof—of the Trinity is one of the main reasons traditional Judaism and Christianity separated. The theology surrounding a triune God drew a clear line in the sand for the Pharisees and rabbis at Yavneh, where the Jewish religious leaders created today's Rabbinic Judaism. Historians and scholars may argue that the Trinity doctrine was not prominent enough to be a factor for those Jewish leaders in AD 90, as the earliest written references to the Trinity were not until the works of Ignatius of Antioch, around AD 110.[4] However, the concept of the Trinity did not originate with the early church fathers but from Jesus Himself when He commanded us in the Great Commission to "go therefore and make disciples of all nations, baptizing them in the name of *the Father and of the Son and of the Holy Spirit*, teaching them to observe all things I have commanded you" (Matt. 28:19–20, emphasis added).

His is the first depiction of the Trinity in the New Testament, but it is not the only one. Peter greeted believers scattered throughout the ancient world "according to the foreknowledge of God the Father, through sanctification by the Spirit, for obedience and sprinkling with the blood of Jesus Christ" (1 Pet. 1:2). Paul concluded his letters to the Corinthians by writing, "The grace of the Lord Jesus Christ, and the love of God, and the communion of the Holy Spirit be with you all" (2 Cor. 13:14). And the apostle John gives possibly the clearest explanation of the Trinity in his first letter: "There are three who testify in heaven: the Father, the Word, and the Holy Spirit, and the three are one" (1 John 5:7).

The mystery of the Trinity is that God exists multidimensionally as Father, Son, and Holy Spirit, yet He is still one. We see this truth evident as far back as the creation story, in which Moses said "the Spirit of God was moving over the surface of the water" and then recounted a Creator God (Father) speaking out the creative Word (Jesus, the Son) to bring things into existence (Gen. 1:1–3). When God desired to make humans, He said, "Let *us* make man in *our* image, after *our* likeness" (v. 26, emphasis added).

If God is just a singular God, as traditional Judaism claims, then who is the "us" He addresses, and why would He use a collective "our"? Did God have a "senior moment" and forget He was alone? I have read Jewish commentaries in which rabbis teach that the Lord was speaking to the angels in heaven. But the truth is that we are not made in the image of angels, which would have to be the case if He were including them as the "us." The very next verse in Genesis 1

proves that we are made in the image of God, not of angels (in fact, it
states this twice to reiterate the point): "So God created man in His
own image; in the image of God He created him; male and female
He created them" (v. 27). Clearly God was speaking to Himself when
He said, "Let us make man in our image, after our likeness" (v. 26).

Why, then, would God feel a need to speak to Himself? Was He
lonely and just needed to hear His own voice? Of course not! The
answer is found in the mysterious truth that within God there is relationship. Scripture clearly states that God is love (1 John 4:8). By
definition, love requires a recipient to receive that love; it needs an
object. If God has always existed before anything was created, and
by definition He is love, then wouldn't there have to be an object receiving that love? Otherwise, He would not be consistent with His
own nature. The truth is, the Father God loved the Son God, who
also has always been. Some Bible translations say the Son is "in the
bosom of the Father" (John 1:18, NKJV); others say He is "near to the
Father's heart" (NLT). I like how the New International Version describes the mystery of this relationship: "No one has ever seen God,
but the one and only Son, who is himself God and is in closest relationship with the Father, has made him known."

Even the Tanakh depicts this relationship by describing the closest thing we have to reflect it on earth: marriage. From its earliest
parts the Torah commanded, "Therefore a man will leave his father
and his mother and be joined to his wife, and they will become one
flesh" (Gen. 2:24). A man and a wife, two separate persons, will join
together and become one. This is the same picture of God the Father
and God the Son! They join together to form a compound unity
rather than a singular unity. Within the Godhead exists a compound
unity between the Father, Son, and Holy Spirit, who holds it together.
Each exalts the other in a perfect cycle of pure love and fellowship.

GOD IN FLESH

You may have noticed that many of the scriptures referred to in this
chapter that describe Jesus' sonship and His equality with God

are from the Book of John. I believe it is no fluke that the apostle whom many say was closest to Jesus went out of His way to explain Jesus' deity and what it means. Under the Holy Spirit's inspiration and throughout his Gospel, John unpacked the timeless mystery of the Trinity, which may have been a deliberate attempt to legitimize Yeshua as Messiah to the very Jewish leaders who had Him killed. Given that both John and all the leaders were Jews, it is possible the apostle wanted to explain such concepts to overcome the traditional Jewish paradigm that prevented them from believing in Jesus as God's Son.

Before I end this chapter, however, I would like to mention one more mystery that posed a problem for the Jewish leaders of Jesus' time and those forming a new Judaism at the Council of Yavneh around AD 90. Once again, the claims surrounding Jesus as God represented another theological crisis centered on a single question: How could God appear in the flesh?

Believing that Jesus was God meant God had demoted Himself, and this was beyond challenging for the Jewish paradigm. They could not fathom that a holy deity made of spirit—which was thought of as the highest form of existence—would willingly choose to lower Himself by being clothed in human flesh. This would be comparable to Bill Gates opting to live in a slum in Mumbai, or to the Queen of England giving up her crown to work at a brothel in Thailand. To the Jews, it just would not—and should not—happen.

Yet in John's powerful opening to his book, he writes:

> In the beginning was the Word, and the Word was with God, and the Word was God. He was in the beginning with God. All things were created through Him, and without Him nothing was created that was created. In Him was life, and the life was the light of mankind. The light shines in darkness, but the darkness has not overcome it.... *The Word became flesh and dwelt among us*, and we saw His glory, the glory as the only Son of the Father, full of grace and truth.
>
> —JOHN 1:1–5, 14, EMPHASIS ADDED

"*The Word became flesh and dwelt among us.*" Stated another way, God clothed Himself with humanity. He put skin on and, as Eugene Peterson phrases it in *The Message*, "moved into the neighborhood." This concept is difficult for traditional Jews to accept—both today and during Jesus' time—and is yet another reason for the separation of Judaism and Christianity. In my experience, most Jewish people's view of God is so lofty that they believe the idea of Him coming in human form actually degrades God's holiness. The traditional mindset of the Jewish people is that God cannot be intimately known. We can obey Him, but He cannot be known in a personal way.

A story involving a Jewish rabbi whom I know well perfectly illustrates this. My friend was in training to be a rabbi when he visited a Charismatic church. He was so impressed with the way the congregation seemed to have an intimate, even emotional, relationship with the Lord that he went on a quest to know God in the same way. He chose to do this, however, through the path of Judaism.

As this rabbinic candidate progressed in his training, he was given an opportunity at the synagogue to go up to the *bema* (pulpit) one day and speak to the congregation. He shared a few words about his church experience and his newfound inspiration to know God more, and then he returned to his seat. Following the service, the senior rabbi approached my friend and said, "You shouldn't talk about God as if He can be intimately known. We can know about God, but we can't intimately know Him. Our obligation is to simply obey Him and keep His commandments."

What a tragedy that so many Jewish people miss out on a personal relationship with God because they, like the senior rabbi, believe that He has relegated us to simply following His ways yet never really knowing Him. The truth is that God *can* be intimately and personally known, and the Torah itself validates this concept. Exodus 33:11 poignantly describes how "The LORD spoke to Moses face to face, just as a man speaks to his friend."

God created mankind for fellowship with Him—to *know* Him in the same way Moses knew Him as a friend. The Lord continually pursues us for this relationship. History is filled with the stories of men and women who encountered God and, as a result, had their lives forever changed by entering into friendship with Him. The reality is that God so desires this relationship that He was willing to come in the flesh to meet us face to face.

In Genesis 18 we find the story of Abraham encountering God in such a way: "The Lᴏʀᴅ appeared to Abraham near the great oak trees of Mamre while he sat in the tent door in the heat of the day. Abraham lifted up his eyes and looked and saw three men standing across from him. When he saw them, he ran from the tent door to meet them and bowed himself toward the ground" (vv. 1–2).

We do not know how or why, but it seems that Abraham immediately knew these were no ordinary men. Virtually every Bible translation uses the word *men* rather than *angels* or *supernatural beings*, and this is important. Whatever or whoever they were, they were dressed in human flesh.

Genesis 18:1 plainly states that "the Lᴏʀᴅ appeared to Abraham," so we have no reason to believe this was anyone else. Isn't it interesting that Abraham immediately recognized that his visitor was the Lord Himself? After meeting Him, Abraham says, "My Lord, if I have found favor in Your sight, do not pass by Your servant. Please let a little water be brought and wash your feet and rest yourselves under the tree. I will bring a piece of bread so that you may refresh yourselves. After that you may pass on, now that you have come to your servant" (Gen. 18:3–5).

The original Hebrew for verse 1 immediately identifies the Lord as יהוה, pronounced "yud-hey-vav-hey" and written as YHVH (Yahweh). This four-letter word is what is called the tetragrammaton and is God's name throughout the Hebrew Bible—a name most Jews throughout history have viewed as so holy it should not be spoken aloud.

It is also certain that Yahweh was in human form, standing right before Abraham. Whether He was one or three under the oaks of Mamre makes no difference for our discussion, though many would argue this is another case of finding the Trinity in the Tanakh because there were three men. What is important for us to see is that

God came to man in human flesh. As far back as Genesis 18 we find God choosing to "demote" Himself by coming to earth in the form of a man (or men).

Theologians call this a theophany, which simply means a preincarnate appearance of Christ—an instance where Jesus showed Himself before actually being born as a baby. Take a moment to think about that: Who else but God could exist before being born? Only the Lord could do such a thing!

Two thousand years after visiting Abraham in the flesh, Jesus once again visited humanity dressed as one of us. Just as He did with Israel's father in Genesis 18, He walked, talked, ate, drank, and did all the things humans do. God came *in the flesh*. Jesus, God's Son, was Emmanuel—meaning "God with us."

Christians accept Jesus' deity, His Sonship within the Trinity, and His incarnation as truths. They are foundational elements of our Christian theology. But for the Jews of Jesus' time, the Nazarene's claims were too much. With hardened hearts and without divine revelation of the Scriptures, they refused to see the Messiah living before them. His claims represented a theological crisis too great to overcome. So when the Jewish leaders formed a new Judaism to unite a reeling, nationless, and scattered people, they had to draw a line in the sand: Jesus was not nor could not be the Son of God.

Sadly their theological defiance has lasted well beyond their own lifetimes. To this day Israel is still rejecting Jesus as its Messiah.

CHAPTER 5

THE CHANGING LAW

MOSES DID NOT descend from Mount Sinai with only two stone tablets but also with a heart full of other commandments God had spoken to Him. Although God Himself wrote the Ten Commandments on the tablets (Exod. 34:28; Deut. 10:4), Moses served as the scribe for many of the other statutes God gave. All together Moses included 613 commandments (according to rabbinic tradition) among his writings. And these, along with the stories of Israel's early history, comprise the Torah.

Yet traditional Judaism believes there is more to God's Law than just the 613 laws Moses wrote down. Rabbinic tradition says that in addition to these laws, there were others he received but did not write down in the Torah and that these were verbally communicated to "seventy of the elders of Israel," as mentioned in Exodus 24. Each generation that followed has continued to pass along this Oral Law, memorizing it alongside the written commandments. To this day Orthodox Jews believe the Law consists of both the Written Law (Torah Shebichtav) and Oral Law (Torah Sheba'al Peh), with both holding equal weight and value as God's Law (Torah).

In the generations between Moses and Jesus, however, the laws passed down orally continued to change. Jewish religious leaders added more and more decrees and regulations on top of what God had already given. What started as an interpretation in one generation became tradition in the next generation—and then law by the very next generation. For example, God gave Moses specific guidelines for what things were considered unclean and could defile a person (e.g., Lev. 11–15). Over time various religious leaders added so much to these defilement laws that they accused Jesus' disciples of defiling themselves by eating bread without first washing their hands the right way (Mark 7:2, 5).

The Pharisees and temple scribes, who served as part of the moral police of the day, challenged Jesus on this and asked why His disciples didn't "live according to the tradition of the elders" (Mark 7:5). His answer was anything but soft:

> Well has Isaiah prophesied of you hypocrites, as it is written: "These people honor Me with their lips, but their hearts are far from Me. In vain do they worship Me, teaching as doctrines the precepts of men." For laying aside the commandment of God, you hold the tradition of men—the washing of pitchers and cups, and many other such things you do.... You full well reject the commandment of God so that you may keep your own tradition.
>
> —MARK 7:6–9

Jesus then continued to highlight other inconsistencies among the religious leaders' traditions, such as making it permissible for people to avoid God's command to honor their parents as long as they promised to "devote" their belongings to God. In all likelihood, their devotion meant more money in the temple fund and toward the priests' salaries.

Despite going against the religious culture of His day, Jesus made a distinction between the laws Moses wrote down and the Oral Law. He did not give them equal weight but instead alluded to the fact that some of the Oral Law was merely the "tradition of men" (Mark 7:8). According to Jesus, this unwritten Oral Law that existed in His day (and is a foundation of today's Orthodox Judaism) was not from His Father at Mount Sinai but from human religious zeal. And sadly these traditions were superseding His Father's original commands. Stated simply, people were losing sight of the main point while paying far more attention to the unnecessary details!

LEADING THE DRIFT

I know of a man who loves to snorkel. He and his wife have gone on many vacations that included hours of exploring pristine waters. Their passion for snorkeling began early in their marriage, when they discovered on their Caribbean honeymoon that it was something they enjoyed doing together. They also encountered a sobering truth during those first swims.

Toward the end of their honeymoon they decided to wake up early and beat the crowds to the beach. They had attended a snorkeling class at their resort and felt confident enough in their swimming abilities to go without a guide. So after putting on sunscreen, fins, snorkels, and masks, they set out to explore a spot their instructor had highlighted the previous day.

What a sight it was! As they floated on the surface, faces down in the water with their backs to the sun, it was as if they had been transported to another world. Fish appeared in all colors—bright blues, purples, oranges, greens, and yellows—and swam only a few feet below them. The larger sea creatures closer to the bottom seemed oblivious to their presence, while entire schools of fish would at times pass within arm's reach. The more time passed, the more these eager snorkelers became one with this mesmerizing aquatic scene.

After what seemed like minutes—but in reality was closer to forty-five minutes—they lifted their heads out of the water to reorient themselves and were shocked. The tide had pulled them so far out that they could no longer see their resort. They did their best to keep calm—the number one rule they had been taught—and came up with a plan to stay together. Fortunately they caught sight of a beach strip a few minutes later, which gave them a set destination to which they could swim. Two and a half hours later they collapsed in their hotel room, utterly exhausted but grateful to have avoided an ending far worse.

This couple had no idea how far they had drifted. They had paid so much attention to the stunning details surrounding them that they literally lost sight of where they had started. In the same way, the religious leaders of Jesus' day had drifted so far from God's original intentions for giving the Law and were completely lost in the details. To make matters worse, they added their own details, which now entangled many of God's people in religious activities and caused them to also drift further and further from His truth.

I hope you can see now why Jesus was so blunt with these religious leaders throughout the Gospels. People ask me why Jesus criticized the Pharisees and scribes while extending such love and compassion to other sinners, and my answer always points to Mark 7 and similar passages of Scripture. The Pharisees were by name "separatists" who looked down on common folk for their inability to follow the Law—both written and oral—as closely as they believed it commanded. But interestingly enough, they could not keep every law themselves. Jesus said they laid heavy burdens on people that they themselves did not keep (Matt. 23:4).

They, along with the temple scribes, priests, and elders, thought of themselves as God's representatives, and they took seriously their role as keepers of both His Law and, ultimately, Jewish culture. In their religious zeal, however, they had created a complex system of man-made traditions that were far from the shoreline of the Torah. Jesus exposed their hypocritical hearts because not only had they personally drifted far from God's heart, but they also were causing countless others to do the same; this was what stirred Jesus' righteous anger.

WHEN COMMENTARY BECOMES LAW

Sadly we know the Jewish religious leaders of Jesus' time did not change their course when Yeshua confronted them but instead grew in their hatred for Him. Even after Jesus' death they continued to drift further from keeping the main point of God's Law in sight for the Jewish people, choosing rather to pile on more traditions. The temple's fall in AD 70 gave leadership an opportunity to return to God's truths and honor His heart above their own traditions.

Unfortunately the exact opposite happened. As mentioned in previous chapters, those who assembled at the Council of Yavneh in AD 90 were determined to unify the Jewish people around a new Judaism, and the identity of this movement centered on new additional traditions, customs, and statutes (extrapolations of the Oral Law). These leaders believed that if Jews were continually scattered in the generations to come, then they needed more than just God's Law to hold them together; they needed someone to *explain* the Law.

For countless generations before, the Jewish religious leaders resisted writing down the Oral Law because they believed doing so would eventually make teachers of the Law irrelevant. The Jewish culture valued teachers more than books, but the religious leaders saw that over time this could change as more Jews were forced to integrate into other societies. As this happened, people would often no longer be able to seek out teachers for interpretation of God's Law. And with the Great Revolt and the temple's fall decimating the number of rabbis, the remaining Jewish leaders believed it was finally time to write down the oral laws and traditions in order to preserve the Torah as a whole. Around AD 200, Rabbi Judah the Prince became the first Jew to write down the Oral Law, as well as many other elements of Judaism, and his compilation of sixty-three dissertations (with other rabbis contributing as well) was called the Mishna.[1]

The Mishna quickly became the topical "guidebook" for Jewish living, tackling in extreme detail everything from newlywed life to dietary recommendations to punishment for involuntary manslaughter. For the next two hundred years, rabbis extensively studied the Mishna—perhaps even more than the Torah itself, in part because it was much longer. In AD 400 these rabbis began writing down their own discussions and responses to the Mishna, which they compiled into a volume of commentaries. And more than a century later additional rabbinic discussions were added to create an authoritative commentary on the Mishna.[2]

Together the Mishna (Oral Law) and these rabbinical commentaries—a massive volume of works that totals almost three thousand double-sided pages—became known as the Talmud, which has become the centerpiece of Jewish study today.[3] Although the Torah is still honored as God's Law, the Talmud is often given just as much weight and, dare I say, far more time and attention. Rabbinic students in *yeshiva* (seminary) today spend much of their time studying the Talmud.

A GROWING GAP

When rabbis write commentaries about commentaries that were originally written to respond to other commentaries about something, then it does not take a genius to predict that the original *something* will change over time. So it is in Jewish history, as God's original message to His people often lies buried under a thick layer of interpretations and commentaries. God's truths do not change, but sadly they have often been viewed throughout history as pieces of art up for scrutiny rather than living authority. As a result, interpretation of the truth has trumped the truth itself and become the centerpiece of Jewish culture.

Again, Jesus railed against the Jewish leaders of His day for elevating such "traditions of men" over God's ways. His followers—all Jewish, at first—were ostracized by their own people for not following all these traditions. Then, when the church became more Gentile, these additional laws began to further cement a growing distance between Judaism and those who followed Jesus. Increasingly, following Yeshua HaMashiach somehow became "less Jewish."

At the same time, Christianity was also getting further and further away from its original Jewish roots and becoming a religion rather than a grassroots movement. We cannot overlook this fact, for if we do, it becomes far too easy to point fingers at the Jewish religious leaders as the sole cause of the growing divide between Judaism and Christianity. And that, in fact, is *exactly* what Satan used in the early church to create division between Jewish and Gentile believers in Jesus.

We have already discussed at length Jesus' Jewishness. We have also discussed how every root of Christianity is planted in that

Jewishness. We who call ourselves followers of Christ—Christians—have a Jewish Lord who came and lived among Jewish people. Our salvation is from, for, and to the Jew first (John 4:22; Rom. 1:16).

But as first- and second-century Jewish leaders made it more difficult for their fellow Jews to follow Jesus, and as God's plan to reach the Gentile world exploded, the church became less Jewish in number and more Gentile in culture. The greater the gap between Gentile and Jewish believers, the more opportunity there was for the same type of distortion that occurred with the evolution of Jewish Law (moving away from God's original commandments toward human traditions). Many of the early Gentile Christians launched their education by attending synagogue (as you will read about more in chapter 7), and yet within only a few decades, this way of learning about the God of Israel—and about the foundational elements of their faith—completely vanished for non-Jews.

Just as God's truths were being buried by man-made tradition from Jewish leaders, the details of Jesus' death were slowly being covered up with layers of Gentile revisionist history. Non-Jews relaying the facts surrounding Jesus' crucifixion to other non-Jews began adding an additional layer of disdain toward the Jewish religious leaders. They were easy targets. After all, they had opposed Jesus more than anyone else and were the only group He spoke against. They were largely responsible for Jesus' death. But just *how* responsible were they? This question added fuel to a slow-building fire that was about to explode into flames of full-blown anti-Semitism. Within only a few generations these leaders—and soon all Jews—would commonly be called "Christ-killers."

THE "PROBLEM" OF JOHN

How could this happen so quickly? Though there are many reasons for the rise of animosity toward the Jewish people, one can be rooted in, of all places, the Gospel of John.

It is without a doubt that John, the Jewish "disciple whom Jesus loved," was not anti-Semitic. Yet his written account of Jesus' life at times casts an undeniably negative shadow upon the Jewish people. No other Gospel writer used the term "the Jews" the way John did, which has stirred up a misunderstanding that to this day continues to be used to defend hatred toward Jewish people.

In John 5 the apostle tells the amazing story of Jesus healing a man by the pool of Bethesda. Lame for thirty-eight years, this man was suddenly able to walk after Jesus commanded him to rise from his mat. The healing, however, was on Shabbat, which caused a stir among the Jewish religious leaders, who wanted to kill Jesus.

The story in John 5 is consistent with similar instances of healings, and with other Gospel accounts of the Jewish religious leaders' ongoing hatred for Jesus—except for one major thing: John doesn't call them religious leaders; he simply calls them "the Jews."

> The man departed and told *the Jews* that it was Jesus who had healed him. So *the Jews* persecuted Jesus and sought to kill Him, because He had done these things on the Sabbath day.
> —JOHN 5:15–16, EMPHASIS ADDED

Was this an oversight on John's part? Did he mean to say "the Jewish religious leaders" or "the Pharisees" or the often-used "Pharisees and scribes"? Surely he didn't mean *all* the Jews. And yet in John 7:1 he writes, "After these things Jesus walked in Galilee. He would not walk in Judea, because *the Jews* were seeking to kill Him" (emphasis added). Again in John 10:31: "Again *the Jews* took up stones to stone Him" (emphasis added). And at the crucial point of Jesus' crucifixion—where surely John would understand the implications of failing to distinguish between those who initially arrested Jesus and an entire race of people—still the apostle writes, "From then on, Pilate tried to release Him. But *the Jews* cried out, 'If you release this Man, you are not Caesar's friend. Whoever makes himself a king speaks against Caesar!' ... 'Away with Him! Away with Him! Crucify Him!'" (John 19:12, 15, emphasis added).

Something is off here. John had to have known that his use of the term "the Jews" would result in anti-Semitism, right? Was he not inspired by the Holy Spirit to write this? What happened?

This "mistake" is repeated throughout John's Gospel no fewer than *seventy-one* times![4] Given that, it is safe to say it was no mistake. So what is going on?

The answer lies partly in understanding the timing and context of John's writing. The earliest possible date John could have written his Gospel is around AD 70, either right before or immediately after the temple's destruction. Some scholars date the Gospel as late as the turn of the century. Either way, we know John wrote during a time of tremendous upheaval within Judaism, when a handful of religious and political groups were vying to put their imprint on the Jewish people's future identity. These groups were often in conflict with each other, and among them were the rabbinical leaders who eventually constructed the beginnings of a "new Judaism" at the Council of Yavneh in AD 90.[5] As discussed earlier, some of these were the sons and grandsons of the very leaders who had schemed to kill Jesus. Therefore, John's negative portrait of "the Jews" in his Gospel was a direct result of a conflict within the larger Jewish community. His readers most likely would have been able to distinguish whom John was talking about when he used the original Greek term *hoi Ioudaioi*, or what most Bible versions simply translate as "the Jews."

Hoi Ioudaioi can mean "the Jews" in general, but it can also more specifically mean "the Judeans," and this was what the religious leaders who so fiercely hated Jesus were called during John's time.[6] At times John intentionally casts a negative light on "the Jews" because he is referring specifically to the religious leaders of his day. Yet not every mention of *hoi Ioudaioi* is negative. At least twice the context is positive, while in several other places it remains neutral. Ultimately we must determine whom John was referring to by the context of each occurrence of *hoi Ioudaioi*.

John was a Jew, as were the other disciples. His Gospel is the only one that includes Jesus' declaring, "Salvation is of the Jews" (John 4:22). It also specifically mentions that Jesus was crucified on the Passover, a Jewish holiday. And in John 10:22 the Gospel writer shows us Jesus celebrating Chanukah, the Feast of Dedication. These and other instances prove that John was not anti-Semitic, nor was he using the term *hoi Ioudaioi* to speak disparagingly of the entire Jewish nation. Again, he was referring specifically to the Judean religious leadership, who positioned themselves as the Jewish leaders during the time of his writing.

If this seems a little confusing, let me give you a modern-day example that might help clarify. The New Testament calls all believers in Jesus Christ priests (1 Pet. 2:9; Rev. 1:6). However, in the Christian culture, we also call the religious leaders in the Catholic Church priests. If I were to use the word *priests* in a conversation with you, you would know which group I was referring to by the context of our conversation, even though I was using the exact same word. It is the same way with John's use of the phrase "the Jews" throughout his Gospel.

Unfortunately we cannot help but read John's Gospel (and its use of the term "the Jews") through a cultural filter of two thousand years of anti-Semitic history—what some have called "the longest hatred."[7] Because of the historical connotations the word *Jew* has, it is virtually impossible for us to view that term today the way John did when he originally used the term *hoi Ioudaioi*. Words have power, particularly when history and stereotypes are added to their meaning. And perhaps few terms over history have been as loaded as the word Jew.

A LOADED TERM

My childhood neighborhoods were mostly Jewish, as I explained in the introduction of this book. However, when my family moved to one particular city, the neighborhood where we lived included more Gentiles. Our neighbors to the left were Jewish, but the man who lived to the right of our house was Gentile.

Shortly after we moved into our new home, my dad decided to build a pool in the backyard, so we hired a contractor. The contractors came out to survey the land and determined that they would have to cut down a few trees to make room for the pool and patio.

Our house backed up to a large wooded area, as did the houses of our neighbors on both sides, so this was expected.

When the contractors chopped down a few trees for the pool, they accidentally removed a tree that was technically on the property of our Gentile neighbor. Keep in mind, this was far from the only tree this neighbor had on his property; there were dozens of others. But when this man discovered that his tree had been cut down, he filed a lawsuit against us. The amount he sued us for included the cost of a tree—exactly the same size and type as the one accidentally removed—being flown in by helicopter, lowered, and replanted.

As you might expect, this extreme response upset my parents. The tree getting cut down had been an honest mistake, and because it was one tree out of an entire backyard full of trees, no real damage had been done. But it apparently did not matter to our neighbor. Obviously the lawsuit made living next to him tense.

Months later, in the midst of this drama, my friends and I were swimming in the new pool. The neighbor suing us walked up to the fence that surrounded our pool area and began staring at us. He just stood there, looking at us, without saying a thing. I am not proud to say that, being the smart-aleck kid I was at the time, I asked him if he wanted to come in for a dip. He looked straight at me and said, "Is that a little Jewish humor?"

"Why are you prejudiced against Jews?" I asked.

"Just kikes," he replied and walked away.

As you can imagine, I have faced other instances of racism since then and am well aware of the racist stereotypes thrown upon the Jewish people. I have felt the sting as I overheard people make comments such as "Man, he's such a Jew" or "I tried to Jew her down on the price." Not everyone who uses these phrases realizes how culturally insensitive they are, and yet I find it fascinating how loaded the term *Jew* has become.

For example, try flipping the tables by replacing the word *Jew* with *Christian*, as in, "Man, he's such a Christian." There is a completely different connotation, isn't there? You are more likely to mean the person is kind or selfless or compassionate or saintly. Even with

Christianity becoming a pop-culture target in the Western world these days, the term Christian still carries a far more positive undertone than Jew.

Where do these connotations come from? From two millennia stained with anti-Semitism. And it is difficult to wipe away the cultural residue of centuries-old accepted racism, just as it is difficult to read John's Gospel—and in particular his use of the term "the Jews"—through glasses not already smeared by anti-Semitic residue.

The growing Gentile church of the first few centuries had the same problem. Despite John's Gospel being so "pro-Jewish"—again, his is the only account that states "salvation is of the Jews" (4:22) or mentions Jesus' Jewish burial (19:40), for example—still the church began to associate all Jews with the deeds of the Jewish religious leaders.[8] Eventually the term "Christ-killer" entered Gentile vocabulary, and within a few generations Jewish people as a whole were held responsible for murdering God's Son. (Somehow the Romans were acquitted from their part in Jesus' crucifixion, proving how powerfully racism can blind people to the truth.)

CHRISTIAN ANTI-SEMITISM

It would be impossible to document all the anti-Semitic teachings, actions, movements, and crusades that have transpired throughout church history. Obviously this is not a history book; otherwise I would spend chapters walking through the progression of Christian hatred toward the Jews. But it is also impossible to overlook the damage some of the early church fathers such as Augustine, Ambrose, Jerome, and John Chrysostom caused with their anti-Semitic views.

You may not know these names, much less be aware of how these men have impacted the church today. And yet not only has their perception of the Jewish people shaped Western culture and history, but I would venture to say it has likely impacted you whether you know it or not. How we view the world is dictated by our past and the cultures in which we were raised, and this is no different in a spiritual sense. We typically perceive the things of God based upon the spiritual atmospheres we were raised in, both from our church and our family background. For example, in the Jewish community, drinking wine is about celebration, but for those who come from a Baptist or Pentecostal background, drinking wine may be seen as a terrible sin. As a believer, your view on drinking has most likely been shaped by whatever spiritual climate you came from, even if you have never considered this.

In the same way, many Christians are unaware of how their perspectives of the Jewish people have been negatively influenced by their spiritual environment. I want to show you not only how some of the "fathers of the faith" have influenced church history and present-day church culture but also how they may be shaping your views on the Jewish people today. Two of the most important individuals in church history concerning this are John Chrysostom and Martin Luther. These men are a small sample of powerful figures in church history who have had great influence on Christian culture. Although they taught and contributed many good things to Christendom, they were also deeply anti-Semitic, and their anti-Semitism grieved God, misled the church, and perhaps has affected your own spiritual environment.

Chrysostom was the bishop of Antioch, one of the five major hubs of the early church. This was an extremely influential post. (See Acts 11:19 and 22, 13:1, and 18:22.) Chrysostom was appointed there in the late fourth century and gained popularity for his bold, eloquent, yet straightforward preaching. He was unafraid to call out abuses of wealth and power (which earned him several enemies and eventually led to his death), and he used much of his personal resources to care for the poor and build hospitals.[9] Yet despite many admirable things he taught and did, Chrysostom also accelerated the growing anti-Semitic movement within Christendom with his vitriolic sermons and writings against the Jewish people, whom he claimed were all "children of the devil" (to misapply John 8:44). The man many call "the early church's greatest preacher" went so far as to label Jews as "dogs," "pigs," "beasts…fit for killing," and souls possessed by demons—and this from one of the major influencers of the early Gentile church![10]

We do not know all the reasons why Chrysostom attacked the Jewish people from his pulpit so openly and harshly. But while some of the patriarchs of the Christian faith took part in widening the gap between followers of Jesus and the very people from which He came, Chrysostom solidified the divide. Yet perhaps the individual who did the most harm in terms of instilling an anti-Jewish mind-set into the modern church is Martin Luther, the founder of the Protestant Reformation that swept Europe during the sixteenth century.

The Reformation began in 1517 when Luther, a Catholic priest, rebelled against the Catholic Church because he felt it was not teaching the truth. The Church at the time was, in a nutshell, selling salvation for money by having its constituents purchase indulgences (sacraments that the Church claimed would pardon or reduce a person's punishment for sinning). Luther argued that salvation was by grace through faith alone. He recognized the errors of the Catholic Church and admirably broke away by posting a copy of his defiant Ninety-Five Theses to the doors of Castle Church in Wittenberg. That moment marked history and created an entirely new branch of Christianity.

Luther became the founder of the Protestant movement, which today includes thousands of different denominations, including Baptist, Methodist, Pentecostal, Lutheran, and Presbyterian. Simply put, his fingerprints can be traced to the beliefs of *billions* of Christians over the past five hundred years. And here is why that is so important: within twenty-six years of posting his Ninety-Five Theses, Martin Luther went from being sympathetic to the Jewish people to calling for mass persecution against them.

In a 1523 tract called *That Jesus Christ Was Born a Jew,* Luther criticized the Catholic Church for its treatment of the Jewish people, and he called believers to reach out to them with the gospel in love and kindness, reminding his readers that "the Jews are of the lineage of Christ."[11] When his attempts to convert Jews failed, however, the German leader made a radical about-face that shaped history. In

1543, only three years before his death, Luther published the deeply
anti-Semitic book *The Jews and Their Lies*, in which he compared the
Jewish people to rats, worms, and pigs, and he wrote at length about
their ties to the devil. He searingly declared that rabbis should be
flailed and forbidden to preach, that synagogues and Jewish schools
should be burned down, and that Jewish houses should be destroyed
and all Jews put under one roof.[12]

Luther's influence at that time went far beyond his Ninety-Five
Theses or his opinions of the Catholic Church. His theology became
the basis for the entire Protestant church movement, and with that
his anti-Semitism became part of the movement's heritage. To this
day the denomination named after Luther, the Lutherans, carries
what I believe is wrong and anti-Semitic theology. In other denominations the seeds of Luther's faulty beliefs grew into replacement
theology, which claims that the Jewish people forfeited their position
as God's chosen people, have been "replaced" by the Gentile church,
and therefore now serve no purpose in God's future plans.

I see traces of Luther's anti-Semitism throughout the evangelical
world today. Not long ago I traveled to Israel with a group of pastors
from many different denominations. Most of these pastors had never
been to the Holy Land before and were thrilled to learn more in person about the Jewish roots of their faith. During a meal one night I
was sharing my testimony and discussing what happens when Jewish
people encounter Jesus when a pastor jokingly said, "Well, Paul met
Jesus and came away with pork on his breath!"

I did not find it funny. Whether that pastor knew it or not, his
statement carried the same insensitive, offensive sting of anti-
Semitism that has been allowed to fester in too many churches. And
sadly its roots in the global body of Christ can be traced back to patriarchs such as Luther, Chrysostom, and others from the church's
earliest days. When you think about it, the idea is preposterous:
How can Gentiles who have been grafted into God's kingdom on account of the Jewish people through a Jewish Messiah respond with
hatred toward Jews? It seems ridiculous, and yet two thousand years
of church history prove it to be the reality.

Although each church father had his reasons for such misguided hatred, much of the division the church fathers brought between Christianity and Judaism can still be traced back to issues surrounding the Law that God gave Moses. Around AD 50 the Council of Jerusalem decided that Gentile believers could be part of this Jewish movement without having to keep the Law and become Jewish. (We will discuss this monumental decision in the next chapter.) This opened up the floodgates for an influx of Gentile believers, as Jewish missionaries inadvertently began to "downgrade" the Jewish laws and commandments while highlighting God's grace extended to all humanity through Jesus Christ. As the church became more Gentile over the next two generations, this led to major questions surrounding the Torah. If God allowed into His kingdom those who did not live according to the Torah, then what purpose did it serve? If Gentiles could be saved without keeping the Law, then what function did it have at all in the church, whether one was Jewish or Gentile?

These and other issues surrounding God's Law began to divide the early church, which was already experiencing heavy persecution from outside. By the end of the first century, many Jewish believers no longer felt part of the global Christian movement that now emphasized a Torah-less faith. Though some Jewish Christians formed their own communities, many forsook "the Way" amid mounting pressure and increasing anti-Semitism. They never could have imagined that the very people who had been "grafted in" to their tree would, in turn, cut them off from what was now becoming a growing tree of religion.

CHAPTER 6

INCLUSION OF THE GENTILES

A FEW YEARS AGO my wife, Cynthia, and I were considering relocating to a different city. We had talked about it and wanted to do it for years before, and the time had come for us to make the move. So we began looking for houses in the city where we would relocate. After a few weeks of searching, we finally found a home that we liked. It was somewhat secluded, had a small pond, and seemed like a perfect fit for us, so we met with the Realtor and signed the contract to start proceedings to purchase the house.

Immediately after signing the papers, I returned to minister at our congregation's evening service. When the service was over, I decided to go back over to the house. I sat alone on the bench by the pond and began to pray: "Father, do You want me to buy this house? Can You confirm that this is the right one and that I'm going in the right direction?"

I left not long after that, went back to our apartment, and fell asleep. That night I had a startling and powerful dream. I saw an image of myself at the house, but I was in a stockade with my head and hands trapped between two boards. I felt completely trapped and could not get out, no matter how hard I tried. I awoke still gripped by a sense of being restricted and bound.

This was a powerful image, one that I knew had not originated in my own mind because I never spend time thinking about stockades. I knew the Lord was speaking to me and giving me a clear message: if you buy that house, you will be trapped.

I couldn't call the Realtor fast enough the next morning to cancel the contract.

Throughout history God has used dreams and visions to change not only people's minds but also their lives. In the Tanakh He spoke to Abraham in a vision and told him that his descendants would be as numerous as the stars in the sky (Gen. 15:1–5). He warned Abimelek, the king of Gerar, in a dream to not touch Sarah and take her for a wife because she was already married to Abraham, which preserved her future as the mother of Israel (Gen. 20:1–7). The Lord gave Joseph prophetic dreams that, though tested through many unjust circumstances, eventually came to pass when he became Egypt's second-in-command (Gen. 37).

Likewise in the B'rit Hadashah, God used a dream to tell Jesus' earthly father, Joseph, to go ahead and wed Mary even though she was pregnant (Matt. 1:20). (The Lord then used dreams twice more to direct the couple and keep Jesus safe.) During Saul's dramatic conversion, God had to give Ananias a powerful vision for him to help the feared man of Tarsus who had persecuted hundreds of believers (Acts 9:10–16). But perhaps no dream or vision has had as powerful and long-lasting an effect on the non-Jewish world as the one Peter experienced on the rooftop of a house while waiting for lunch.

To properly understand Peter's vision, we have to rewind a bit and look at the situation God orchestrated. The account in Acts 10 begins by introducing us to Cornelius, a man whom Scripture goes out of its way to show as worshipping the Jewish God. Not only did Cornelius lead his entire household in fearing the one true God of Israel (already an anomaly for someone living in Caesarea's polytheistic, Roman-influenced culture), but he also "gave many alms to the people" (likely poor Jewish people) and "continually prayed to God" (v. 2). It is possible Cornelius even lived like a Jew, following the ethical code of the Tanakh, attending synagogue, and observing Shabbat.

There was one problem, though: he was not Jewish but Italian. To make matters worse, he worked for the enemy as a Roman centurion. By any Jewish standard, he was a Gentile and therefore unclean.

Despite these attributes—or maybe *because* of them—an angel of God appeared to Cornelius in a vision (yet another one!), instructing him to summon Peter. He immediately obeyed and sent two men to find this man. That is where we pick up the rest of Luke's account in Acts:

> The next day as they went on their journey and drew near the city, Peter went up on the housetop to pray about the sixth hour. He became very hungry and desired to eat. But while they prepared a meal, he fell into a trance and saw heaven opened, and a vessel like a great sheet, tied at the four corners, descending to him, and let down to the earth. In it were all kinds of four-footed animals of the earth and wild beasts and reptiles and birds of the air. Then a voice came to him, "Rise, Peter; kill and eat."
>
> Peter said, "Not at all, Lord. For I have never eaten anything that is common or unclean."
>
> The voice spoke to him a second time: "What God has cleansed, do not call common."
>
> This happened three times. And again the vessel was taken up into heaven.
>
> —ACTS 10:9–16

When Peter received this vision, he initially had no idea what it meant. If he were like many of us, he could have shrugged off what happened and chalked it up to being deliriously hungry. But God made sure that did not happen. While Peter was brewing over what the vision could have meant, the Lord told him to go downstairs and meet Cornelius' servant, who had just arrived, because He had set up this situation. Peter obeyed and, taking a big step of faith, ended up in the Gentile home of Cornelius.

Peter's first move upon entering the household is not exactly the kind of thing taught in an International Etiquette 101 class. He opened his mouth and essentially announced to his Gentile hosts, "Hey, guys, you know I'm not supposed to be here because, well, I'm clean, and you're not. I'm special—a Jew, you know, one of God's chosen people—and you guys are, well, not. You're unclean."

Talk about a cultural icebreaker! Thankfully Peter did not stop there.

"But God has shown me not to call any man common or unclean" (Acts 10:28).

I cannot overemphasize the magnitude of these words and what

they have meant to all humanity ever since. In just a short statement Peter introduced the idea that God Himself was now merci-
fully opening the gates of heaven to all. Almost fifteen hundred years
earlier the Lord had given the Jewish people strict commandments
to live sanctified, set apart, and "cleansed" from the filth of the rest
of the world. God gave the Law in Moses' time to a specific people so
that through them He could display His holiness to the nations. He
did not give these exclusive commands because He hated Gentiles
or was racist. In fact, within the same Law, He gave specific instructions on how to take in foreigners with kindness and compassion.
He wanted Israel to be a refuge for those who sought safety in the
one true God. He loved the foreigner but hated the godlessness that
had consumed most of their nations, and so He desired a people set
apart for Him as representatives of His kingdom.

Unfortunately the Jewish people often disobeyed God's commandments, intermarried with idol-worshipping peoples, integrated
into their societies, and adapted the worst parts of their cultures.
Throughout the Old Testament this routinely led to the fall of the
Jewish people. During Jesus' time they suffered some of the consequences of this, living as a nationless people under the oppression of
the Roman Empire.

Still they were allowed to keep their Jewish culture—including
their religious customs—and as a result most adhered to the idea
of living secluded from the rest of the unclean, Gentile world. That
meant on a daily basis the average Jew tried not to associate with
anyone who was not Jewish. At times this was unavoidable, such as
when they were forced to interact with Roman authorities or visiting foreigners. But for the most part, to be a Jew meant your entire
world was insulated from Gentile defilement.

Suddenly, with one rooftop vision, Peter received the divine revelation that God no longer considered a Gentile unclean just because
he or she was not Jewish. Because of the sacrifice of His Son, Yeshua
HaMashiach, God opened the gates of His kingdom to now include
Gentiles as well. He was the only One with the right to do this, and

through the ultimate fulfillment—Jesus—of His own Law, He had made the unclean clean.

A SUPERNATURAL, SILENCING SIGN

As you can imagine, not every Jewish follower of Jesus took to this right away. When Peter later returned to the believers in Jerusalem, they immediately scolded him: "You went in and ate with uncircumcised men!" (Acts 11:3). The idea of mingling with unclean Gentiles went against *everything* the Jewish nation stood for—all their moral standards, theologies, and daily codes of living. So what Peter told them was truly revolutionary!

God knew how difficult this would be for them to accept, and He also knew it would take something undeniable—something supernatural—to prove to the Jewish believers that what Peter was submitting was truth from God. That is why the Lord also sent His Holy Spirit to Cornelius and his household.

If Peter had returned to his fellow Jews after visiting Cornelius and simply relayed that God had OK'd him setting foot in a Gentile home, I doubt it would have had the same impact. But instead, Peter had no choice but to tell them what had surprised him as well: not only had these Gentiles been deemed clean by the Lord, but they had also been baptized in the Holy Spirit!

God's gift of the Holy Spirit was something that up to that point had been received only within the exclusively Jewish movement. Remember, the original church was 100 percent Jewish. Not a single Gentile was among those who followed Jesus after He ascended to heaven. The glorious account of Pentecost in Acts 2 is filled with phrases that show how entirely Jewish this event was. Those who heard the disciples first speaking in tongues were "Jews, devout men, from every nation under heaven…both Jews and proselytes" who spoke in various languages (vv. 5, 10). (The proselytes were non-Jews who converted to Judaism.) When Peter preached to the crowds that day, he specifically addressed them as "men of Judea and all you who dwell in Jerusalem" (v. 14), as "men of Israel" (v. 22), and as "brothers" (v. 29). He most certainly would have never said this to Gentiles!

Three thousand people became part of the church on Pentecost, and more continually joined from that point on until the day Peter visited Cornelius. Yet all those who had joined were Jewish. Even those among them who were not born Jewish had converted to become Jewish by Jewish standards. In the mind of every church member, to follow Jesus meant you had to be Jewish.

When the church in Jerusalem heard Peter's report of these Gentiles being baptized in the Holy Spirit, Scripture says they responded with total silence (Acts 11:15, 18). I can tell you as a Jewish believer, that is not very Jewish! Our culture is typically expressive, whether we are celebrating exuberantly or grieving loudly. So a response of silence means something significant has happened. Thankfully we are not left wondering if that "something" in Jerusalem was good. The very next sentence of Scripture says, "And they glorified God, saying 'Then God has granted to the Gentiles also repentance unto life'" (Acts 11:18).

The Jewish believers were literally left speechless because they could not come up with any more arguments against God's decision. Peter said it best when he admitted, "If then God gave them the same gift as He gave us when we believed in the Lord Jesus Christ, *who was I to be able to hinder God?*" (Acts 11:17, emphasis added). Truly we cannot stop God's purposes. When He wants "all men to be saved and to come to the knowledge of the truth," He will have His way (1 Tim. 2:4). That means all classes of people, all races, all people groups, and people from every nation, tribe, and tongue (Rev. 7:9). And thankfully we know His ways are infinitely higher—and better—than ours (Isa. 55:8–9). Hallelujah!

TO BE OR NOT TO BE

As the church continued to grow, the significance of Cornelius' salvation extended far beyond Caesarea into every territory where the kingdom of God was preached and was expanding. Although those in Jerusalem admitted that God had allowed Gentiles to be part of this Jewish faith, few believers actually sought out the non-Jews. Again, we must understand that every Jewish man and woman was accustomed to *not* associating with Gentiles because that is how countless preceding generations had lived. So even as believers were scattered throughout different regions because of persecution, still they were "preaching the word to no one except Jews" (Acts 11:19).

Things were apparently different in Antioch. The intercultural atmosphere of the big city meant Jewish believers had more opportunity to interact with Gentiles. We do not know whether they did; all we know is that the church there began growing so much that the "mother church" in Jerusalem sent Barnabas to help. Eventually he and Paul (formerly Saul) left as missionaries, preaching to both Jews and Gentiles throughout modern-day Turkey and Syria. The incredible success of that first missionary journey meant more Gentiles now believed in Jesus. But as their numbers increased, it raised a question so important that a council was called in Jerusalem around AD 50.

The issue, as recorded in Acts 15, was whether these newly converted Gentiles needed to become Jewish. A Pharisee sect of believers in Jesus (some Pharisees did believe; see John 3:1–10) argued that a non-Jew needed to be circumcised and follow the Torah to have a relationship with the God of Israel. Barnabas and Paul argued adamantly that this was not the case, as evident in God's blessing upon the growing movement of Gentile believers. Much was at stake in the Council of Jerusalem's decision, for if their answer was that non-Jewish believers needed to become Jewish, then the explosive church growth seen from the missionary journeys would certainly dampen.

Allow me to pause for a moment and highlight something. Can you see how drastically times have changed since this debate? Today the tables are turned and the question is whether you can believe in Jesus and still be a Jew. The paradigm is the exact opposite of what it was at the Council of Jerusalem! Back then it was assumed that a follower of Jesus was already Jewish, so the issue in question only

involved non-Jews. They were the outsiders looking in; yet today it is
the Jewish people who are largely on the outside. Christianity is seen
as a Gentile religion, while Judaism is, of course, a Jewish one.

I am living proof that you can follow Jesus *and* be Jewish. In fact, I
cannot think of anything *more* Jewish than following Jesus! I call myself a Jewish Christian. But it is interesting that both Jews and Gentiles ask me the same question today: How can you be a Jew when
you believe in Jesus? Jews assume I am Christian—and therefore
not a Jew—because I follow Jesus. And Gentiles assume I am not a
Christian because I am Jewish. Talk about worlds colliding!

The Council of Jerusalem saw this crash course in the works, but
like me and countless other Messianic Jews, they reconciled the
two under the Holy Spirit's guidance. After Peter and James (Jesus'
brother) offered their opinions, the group reached a conclusion: "For
it seemed good to the Holy Spirit and to us to put on you [Gentiles]
no greater burden than these necessary things: Abstain from food
offered to idols, from sexual immorality, from strangled animals, and
from blood" (Acts 15:28–29).

Why these four things? Because on a practical level, each would
have made it incredibly difficult for Jewish believers to have any fellowship with their Gentile brothers and sisters. These four elements
were major "defilements" according to the Jewish Law, and the Council was simply requesting that Gentile believers honor their Jewish
brothers in the same way that Paul encouraged any follower of Jesus
"not to put a stumbling block or an obstacle in a brother's way" (Rom.
14:13). Using food as an illustration of this principle, Paul stated
it best: "Do not destroy the work of God for the sake of food. All
things indeed are clean, but it is evil for the man who causes someone to fall by what he eats" (v. 20). In general, the Jerusalem believers
gave Gentiles the freedom to live as Gentiles but asked that they abstain from four things that, in the everyday life of a Jewish-Gentile
relationship, would lead a Jewish brother or sister to sin according to
the Law.

ATTACKED FOR ASSOCIATING

I wonder if Peter, James, Barnabas, Paul, and the other believers gathered in Jerusalem knew the ramifications their decision would have. God had already proved He longed for Gentiles to know Him and to have an eternal, saving relationship with Him through His Son. The Holy Spirit was at work throughout the surrounding regions, and thousands of Gentiles were saved. The Jewish believers saw God's extensive plans unfold before their eyes—plans God had revealed to their father Abraham generations before when He said, "I will make you into a great nation…and all peoples on earth will be blessed through you" (Gen. 12:2–3, NIV).

Many Jews in the church embraced their newfound Gentile brothers and sisters, and despite Jews being raised to not associate with unclean Gentiles, they treated them like family. Both the New Testament and historical documents prove that the early church grew in numbers with a spirit of unity and love, to such a degree that nonbelievers recognized those of "the Way" by their extreme compassion and willingness to help those in need.[1] Surely this was a wonderful time for the young body of Christ!

Indeed it was. But unfortunately what began as a glorious time for the church eventually turned into an era of conflict with those outside of it. Although a brand-new era had emerged where Jewish and Gentile believers were living together in unity, the opposition against this new movement continued to escalate.

The Pharisees, Sadducees, and temple leaders continued to persecute the "Nazarenes," as Jewish believers were known, whenever they could. Acts 12:3 briefly mentions that the execution of James under Herod's order "pleased the Jews." Throughout Barnabas and Paul's first missionary journey, Jewish leaders and commoners alike repeatedly tried to sabotage their preaching efforts and eventually stirred up the crowds into such a frenzy that they "stoned Paul and dragged him out of the city, supposing he was dead" (Acts 13:45; 14:2, 5, 19).

In the eyes of traditional Jews, it was bad enough for followers of Yeshua to blaspheme and claim the dead rabbi was Israel's Messiah.

But associating with Gentiles took their "cult" to another level of defilement. How could any group associate with the unclean heathen and still call themselves God's people?

Apparently the Jewish religious leaders were not the only ones attacking Jewish believers for their association with Gentiles. Israel was filled with Jewish nationalistic groups at the time, and among these were radicals who persecuted any Jews connected with Gentiles. We catch wind of the pressure they put on integrated churches when Paul mentions in Galatians how he rebuked Peter in front of the Gentile-filled Antioch church.[2] Apparently Peter had no problem eating with the Gentiles in normal circumstances. But when "those who belong to the circumcision group" arrived, Peter pulled away from the Gentiles and only ate with Jews (Gal. 2:12, NIV). Paul confronted Peter for his "hypocrisy" (vv. 13–14), but the conflict also shows just how much Jewish nonbelievers could influence even those in the early church's leadership by making life miserable for them. Once again, those among the Jewish religious and political leadership were able to use their attacks to further the lie that following Jesus somehow made you "less Jewish."

CURSING JEWISH ENEMIES

Such cultural propaganda reached a climax years later following the Council of Yavneh in AD 90. We have discussed in previous chapters how Pharisees and other religious leaders tried to reunite the Jewish people after this gathering by forming a new Judaism. Because the three pillars of Jewish temple culture—the temple building, sacrifices, and priests—were no longer in the picture, the religious leaders' plan was to create new customs and traditions that would form the core of a new Jewish identity. More specifically, the Pharisees and rabbis came up with new liturgy and prayers.

But these culture shapers were cunning. They had witnessed and continued to witness the great Diaspora—the dispersion of the Jews—taking place as a result of the temple's destruction and Rome enslaving many other Jews. So with a desire to create a new Judaism followed by unified, like-minded Jews, they added within the new liturgy a curse against anyone who did not follow the Pharisees' teaching or who created false teachings—separatists and heretics. Three times a day Jews were to recite this curse as part of the prayer liturgy. Yet what has fascinated historians through the years is the extent to which this "prayer" may have been specifically directed at followers of Christ.

The Birkat ha-Minim was one of many prayers used for benediction during weekday prayer gatherings. What made it unique was its call for divine wrath upon the named "enemies" of Rabbinic Judaism—both inside and outside of Judaism. We do not have dated copies of the original prayer to confirm exactly who those enemies were in the first century during the rise of the church, but we are given clues through later versions such as this one from between the ninth and twelfth centuries:[3]

> For the apostates let there be no hope. And let the arrogant government be speedily uprooted in our days. Let the *nozerim* and the *minim* be destroyed in a moment. And let them be blotted out of the Book of Life and not be inscribed together with the righteous. Blessed art thou, O Lord, who humblest the arrogant.[4]

The mystery that has intrigued scholars surrounds two words: *nozerim* and *minim*. The latter can be translated to mean "heretics," but most studies of the word *nozerim* identify it with the term Nazarenes, which is what Jewish believers in Jesus were called.[5] Early church writings from Epiphanius around AD 374–377 mention Jews cursing fellow Jews who accept Jesus as the Messiah, while letters from Jerome (AD 404–410) mention Jews cursing all Christians, whether Gentile or Jew.[6]

Even if the first- and second-century Jewish liturgy did not contain any curses directed at Gentile believers, we know that the Pharisees and rabbis created a system that intentionally demonized any Jews who chose to follow Yeshua. In fact, some scholars believe the curse specific to the nozerim was added shortly after the Council of Yavneh to keep Jewish believers from the synagogue life.[7]

Scholars can debate the facts surrounding the Birkat ha-Minim, but what is undeniable is the spirit behind such liturgy that loaded prayers with political agendas. Let me remind you of what we discovered in an earlier chapter: These Pharisees and religious leaders were the sons and grandsons of the same leaders behind Jesus' death, whom Jesus described as children of the devil (John 8:44). Their manipulative efforts to control the Jewish culture stemmed from an antichrist spirit at work both during Jesus' life and well into the next century. And to a degree, that evil spirit had some success in pulling the early church apart: first, by ostracizing Jewish believers from their own people and making following Jesus "less Jewish"; and second, by creating a divide between seemingly "defiled" Jewish believers who associated with Gentiles and other Jews who, by not doing so, remained "clean."

As we shall soon see, this Pharisaical spirit behind the new Judaism developed at Yavneh would manifest in new ways during the second century—ways that would lead to an all-out revolt and create further separation between Judaism and Christianity.

CHAPTER 7

THE REVOLTS

T HE COUNCIL OF Jerusalem left a permanent mark on history. Its decision to allow Gentile believers to remain Gentile rather than becoming Jewish changed not only the church but also the entire world from that day forward. The outcome paved the way for a massive influx of Gentile believers and set the stage for the rise of Christianity as a global movement. But I have often wondered how the early church leaders—all Jewish—could so easily accept non-Jews into the fold without fearing that the Jewishness of this Jesus movement would begin to be affected or, dare I say, lost.

The early Jewish believers were, in fact, concerned about losing the Jewishness of their faith. And this is why James concluded his statement by saying, "For Moses has had in every city since early generations those who preach him, being read in the synagogues every Sabbath" (Acts 15:21). What did Moses being preached have to do with Gentiles not becoming Jewish?

It had everything to do with it. James was making a bold statement of faith: "I am absolutely confident these Gentiles who have now come into relationship with the God of Israel *will* get more understanding of who He is, even if they do not become Jewish and follow all our ways." How could Jesus' brother be so assured of this? Because the Torah—Moses' five foundational books revealing who God was—was being read each week. James knew that every time the Tanakh was opened, the God of Abraham, Isaac, and Jacob would be shown. The more Gentiles heard or read the Jewish Bible in the synagogue, the more they would come to know this Jewish God and His ways.

And James was right. When Gentiles were first saved, one of the main sources of their education as followers of Jesus was the synagogue. This was the epicenter for Jewish learning during this era, as rabbis had become the teachers and guardians of the Tanakh. To learn more about following Jesus, then, you needed to know more about the very Law and Prophets He came to fulfill. In Matthew 5:17 Jesus said, "Do not think that I have come to abolish the Law or the Prophets. I have not come to abolish, but to fulfill." Because Jesus was the Tanakh's fulfillment, those who claimed to follow Him would benefit from knowing the Tanakh, even if they were not bound to the Law in the way God's people had previously been.

The Gentile believers of the early church grew in their faith and understanding partly because they were taught about God in the synagogue each week. They were not required to live under the Law, but they wanted to know the Law (and the rest of the Tanakh) to receive greater revelation of God as the Father, Son, and Holy Spirit as revealed through the Hebrew Bible. Scripture indicates that many Gentiles wanted more and more teaching; such was their hunger for knowing the one true God of Israel. For example, after Paul and Barnabas gave an overview teaching of Jewish history in a synagogue in Antioch, Gentiles were waiting at the door as the pair left and "asked that these words might be preached to them the next Sabbath" (Acts 13:42).

Some have questioned whether these Gentiles in Antioch were actually attending the synagogue since Scripture does not make it clear whether they were hearing the apostles' teaching inside with the Jews or waiting outside for the chance to talk with Paul and Barnabas. Either way, we know there were Gentiles who wanted revelation about the God of Israel because they had a designated section in God's temple in Jerusalem called the Court of the Gentiles. The Lord had actually designed His house with Gentiles in mind because He desired for them to come and learn about Him and worship Him. From this we can presume that synagogues were set up in similar fashion, with Gentiles welcomed to learn about the Law of Moses from "those who preach him" (Acts 15:21).

REVOLT TURNS INTO PUNISHMENT

Unfortunately a major turn of events interrupted this beautiful educational process. In AD 66 the First Jewish Revolt (often called the Great Revolt) began with uprisings scattered throughout Palestine. This affected many local synagogues, which would often become places of discourse for nationalist groups to build support in their efforts against Roman oppression. We have already discussed the events of the First Jewish Revolt in chapter 3, but suffice to say it certainly affected many Gentile believers who had gone to the synagogue to learn more about their newfound Jewish-rooted faith. Just as important, however, the uprisings resulted in a harsh punishment that was instrumental in dividing Christianity (including both Jewish and Gentile believers) and Judaism.

When the Revolt ultimately failed and the temple was leveled in AD 70, millions of Jews scattered throughout the Roman Empire in the aftermath. Rome had previously allowed the Jewish people to retain their culture and live as a "separated" people while still under Roman authority. Part of the arrangement included Rome collecting Jewish taxes directly from the temple collections. People would tithe toward the temple's maintenance, and Rome would take a portion of that. But with the Roman government now enraged from the uprisings, and with the temple in ruins, the Jewish people were punished another way.

The fiscus Judaicus was a tax placed upon Jews for being, well, Jewish. It was the epitome of anti-Semitism. Every Jewish man, woman, child, and even slave throughout the Empire had to pay a half shekel to Rome. But to add insult to injury, whereas Jews had previously paid this amount to their temple, now Rome forced them to pay it toward the temple of Jupiter Capitolinus, the center of Roman polytheistic religion.[1] This flew in the face of everything Judaism represented, and Rome knew this. The emperor who first imposed this humiliating tax, Vespasian, did not concern himself with details of exactly which Jews paid the tax. But his successor, Domitian, enforced the tax rigorously and cruelly, beginning around AD 85. One historian documents a ninety-year-old man being inspected in front of a crowd by a Roman official to see if he was circumcised.[2]

Domitian seemed bent on quelling the growing movement of Christians, which was first presumed to be just another Jewish sect but had continued to grow, particularly among non-Jews. First, the emperor expanded fiscus Judaicus to include not only Jews and converted Jews but also those who "lived like Jews" (publicly or not) and those who hid their Jewishness.[3] In short, Emperor Domitian was targeting Gentile and Jewish believers! Then, to make matters worse, he levied an even greater punishment on Gentile Christians. In addition to heavy taxation, any Roman who "drifted into Jewish ways"—namely those who became Gentile believers in the Jewish God—would be executed.[4]

As you can imagine, these punishments drastically changed things for Jewish and Gentile believers, as well as traditional Jews. Where do you think the Romans went first to enforce this taxation? The synagogue—and on Shabbat! This caused many Gentile believers in Jesus to no longer attend synagogue to avoid being taxed. And because they had been permitted by the Council of Jerusalem to follow Jesus yet not become Jewish, many succeeded in escaping Domitian's targeted persecution. Their Jewish believing brothers and sisters, however, could not—and this caused further separation between Gentile and Jewish believers.

FADING JEWISHNESS

Many Gentile believers may have avoided Rome's punishment for following the Jewish Messiah, but it took time for the greater cost of this to surface. Despite increased opposition and persecution, the Gentile church still grew—an amazing testament to the power of the gospel of Yeshua HaMashiach. But because these non-Jewish believers stopped going to synagogues to avoid being taxed, they had less and less information about the God of Israel, about His character and ways, about the past history with His people, about the Jewish holy days, and about many other important things. In short, they had no understanding, no information, and no revelation regarding the Old Testament Scriptures.

Remember, Jesus deemed the Hebrew Bible invaluable when He said, "Do not think that I have come to abolish the Law or the Prophets. I have not come to abolish, but to fulfill" (Matt. 5:17). He defeated Satan by quoting from the Book of Deuteronomy. Jesus revealed that He was the Messiah by referencing various Messianic prophecies about Him in the Old Testament. And He told His disciples that when they mined the Old Testament, they would find treasures "new and old" (Matt. 13:52).

Clearly Jesus placed an importance on His followers learning and knowing the Hebrew Bible. He never intended the Gentile church to be separated from understanding the Hebrew roots of their faith or from the Old Testament Scriptures. He wanted the church to be grounded in the Word, both Old and New Testaments.

I meet many believers today who refer to themselves as "New Testament Christians," meaning they walk in the grace of God to be free from the Law in the same way Paul described. But unfortunately that phrase has also become a mentality among believers—that because we are "New Testament Christians" now, the Old Testament is no longer relevant.

The truth is that New Testament Christians have the same need for knowing the Old Testament truths as the early Christians did. Our faith is based upon these truths! Everything we believe is centered on Jesus being the fulfillment of the Hebrew Bible. So the Old Testament is critical!

Unfortunately the growing Gentile church began to lose sight of this foundation because of many factors we have already mentioned and more (e.g., Roman taxation, death threats, separation from the synagogue, etc.). As a result, the church began to look less and less Jewish. With no Tanakh to read from, no one to explain it (or at least to help guide discussion), and fewer Gentiles attending synagogue, the church relied more on testimonies, experiences, and personal opinions, which opened the door for false doctrine. This is why we find Paul and other New Testament writers addressing so many of these theological issues throughout their letters. The Gentile church, though growing, faced danger not only from outside anti-Christian forces but also from within its own ranks. And within two or three generations—less than one hundred years—the Christian movement would look vastly different than it did in AD 70, when Jewish and Gentile believers were learning how to fellowship together and even attending synagogue together.

EXPELLED BY THEIR OWN

Gentile believers were not the only ones unable to go to the synagogue. While Roman persecution against Jewish Christians increased following the temple's fall, so did the attacks from their fellow Jews. Jewish believers were thrown out of the synagogue, just as Jesus had warned His disciples about: "I have spoken these things to you so that you will not fall away. They will put you out of the synagogues. Yes, the time is coming that whoever kills you will think that he is offering a service to God" (John 16:1–2).

In John's account the disciple also alludes to synagogue expulsion: "For the Jews had already agreed that if anyone confessed that He was the Christ, he would be put out of the synagogue" (John 9:22). Many scholars agree that John intentionally referenced this for his future readers' sake (decades after Jesus' death).[5] Some of those same scholars argue that the Birkat ha-Minim, the curse added to new liturgy after the Council of Yavneh, was intentionally incorporated into the synagogue to weed out any Jewish believers, who would be reluctant to pray such a curse upon their own brothers and sisters in the faith.[6] Whether this is true or not, we know that religious leaders would later begin to openly curse Jesus in the synagogue and blame Him and His followers for some of the persecution they were experiencing as Jews.[7] By the turn of the first century, Jewish believers, now labeled as heretics and sectarians, were officially barred from most synagogues.

Their situation grew worse with another major revolt in Jewish history. When Hadrian became Roman emperor in AD 118, Jews scattered throughout the Empire received a glimmer of hope when he allowed them to return to Jerusalem and granted permission for them to rebuild the temple. Leaders of the new Judaism were ecstatic and immediately began collecting funds for what would have been the third major rebuilding project in the temple's history.[8]

That project never happened, as Hadrian went back on his word and began deporting more Jews. They found out the emperor actually planned to build a Roman temple in Jerusalem over their own temple. After several years passed and the situation worsened under the harsh leadership of Judean governor Tinneius Rufus, many Jews had had enough and plotted another revolt.[9]

Enter Shimon Bar-Kokhba, a charismatic leader whom many believed was the long-awaited Messiah. For those looking for a political leader who would restore the nation of Israel with force, he seemed to have all the right qualifications: he was believed to have descended from David's line, his name meant "son of light" and alluded to a Messianic prophecy about a star, and he was a dictator in every sense who commanded his troops with sheer force and will.[10] He gave Jews everywhere hope when he launched a large-scale assault against weakened Roman forces in AD 132 and captured fifty strongholds in Judea. At that time he also conquered Jerusalem and more than nine hundred other unprotected towns.

Many Jewish believers in Jesus supported the revolt and the notion of fighting Roman oppression once more. And for a brief season this united them with those who had been opposing them. Remember, Judaism was not a singular movement and had not been so for many years. In Jesus' time there were the Pharisees, Sadducees, Essenes, Zealots, and Hellenists, to name just a few. The First Jewish Revolt had wiped out many of those groups, but at the time of this second revolt there were still the Pharisees and a handful of nationalist groups. The Nazarenes (Jewish believers) were seen as one of many factions in Jewish culture, but they were still considered Jews.

When all of Judea claimed that Bar-Kokhba was the Messiah, however, this created a serious dilemma. Most Jewish believers left and were immediately labeled as traitors. They had already been

alienated from synagogue life; now they were excommunicated from
the rest of Jewish life and treated even more harshly. At this point in
Jewish society, to be a Jewish follower of Jesus unofficially meant you
were no longer a Jew.

THE FINAL SEPARATION

Not surprisingly the Bar-Kokhba revolt ultimately failed. After a
three-year war, the Jewish people were once again left scattered, de-
pleted, and despondent. Rome leveled Jerusalem—soldiers literally
plowed it down with a yoke of oxen—and turned it into a pagan city.
Hadrian was so enraged by the Jewish revolts that he forbade Jews
to enter the city, changed Judea's name to Syria Palaestina, and out-
lawed circumcision.[11]

The Jewish believers who would not join the Bar-Kokhba revolt
were from this point on excluded from the traditional Jewish community. A spirit of separation from their own people continued for
the next few hundred years until there arose one of the most significant instigators of the official divide between Judaism and Christianity: Flavius Valerius Aurelius Constantinus Augustus—otherwise
known as Constantine the Great.

The son of a Caesar, Constantine rose through the military ranks
of the Roman Empire to become emperor of its western region in
AD 306. At the time, the empire was divided into three main geo-
graphical sections, each ruled by a separate emperor. By AD 312,
Constantine was well on his way to conquering the other regions
and becoming sole emperor. Yet on the eve of a crucial battle to gain
the throne, Constantine saw a vision of a cross made of light in the
sky and above it the inscription "By this symbol you shall conquer."
Later he dreamed that Jesus appeared to him and commanded him
to make the cross and "use it as a safeguard in all engagements with
his enemies."[12]

What happened that day changed the course of human history.
For three centuries prior, followers of Jesus had been increasingly
persecuted. Yet after Constantine learned more about the Christian

faith—including from his mother, who had converted and who heavily influenced him—he immediately began to implement radical changes throughout the Roman Empire. In February AD 313, his Edict of Milan declared that Christians could worship freely without fear of persecution. Over the next ten years, the Empire shifted from outlawing Christianity to accepting it to fully supporting it—with Constantine enforcing the return of church properties to Christians.[13]

What seemed like a wonderful era for followers of Christ, however, became a nightmare for nonbelieving Jews. The more Constantine embraced this modern, Gentile version of Christianity, the more his hatred for the Jewish people grew. In AD 325 he convened the Council of Nicaea, a gathering of Christian leaders throughout the Roman Empire that produced some of the first foundational doctrines of Christianity as a religion, summarized in the Nicene Creed. Yet the Council also made decisions that further tore Christianity away from its Jewish roots, including establishing Easter as separate from Passover and determining its date by the Roman calendar rather than the Jewish calendar, which had continued to be used to this point.

Deciding a date for Easter may not seem significant at first glance, but Constantine's reasoning behind it reflects the anti-Semitic spirit of the Council. He called the Jews "detestable...wicked men" who were possessed by a "mad spirit." Because they were responsible for killing Jesus, he argued, they were "deservedly afflicted with blindness of soul" and therefore could not be trusted even to accurately date the death of the Savior they rejected.[14]

What would cause a man new to the Christian faith to use such words as *detestable, mad,* and *wicked* to describe the Jewish people? Wouldn't he recognize the Lord as a Jewish Messiah, especially since the Scriptures he had were all Jewish? Clearly there was something else behind Constantine's words.

As we have discovered in previous chapters, the division between Judaism and Christianity had already been growing since the early church's third and fourth generations. Yet Constantine put into words the racist spirit emerging not just between religions but between the *peoples* involved in those faiths—particularly on the side of Christianity. Out of this spirit the entire Jewish race would be cast in a negative light from the Roman throne down to its subjects, which certainly influenced the cultural perspective toward Jews.

With an emperor now on its side, Christianity quickly became a popular faith and by AD 380 was the official religion of the Roman Empire. Constantine's successors continued to make Jews second-class citizens; they were forbidden to own Christian slaves or circumcise their slaves, and they could be put to death for converting a person to Judaism or even persecuting Jews who converted to Christianity.

Meanwhile the Jewish people suffered the wrath of a population now taught to hate them. Additional church councils increasingly demonized the Jewish people, making them the sole enemies and murderers of Jesus. Gentile Christians were taught that His blood remained forever stained upon their hands. The councils went so far as to ban Christians from joining Jews—even fellow believers—in celebrating Passover, and they were not even allowed to receive gifts from them during religious holidays.[15]

Is it any wonder that out of this anti-Semitic culture emerged church fathers such as Augustine, John Chrysostom, and Martin Luther, who so openly voiced their hatred for the Jewish people? Despite all the ways God used them to shape the church, these men were still products of a rising new religion that had the entire Roman Empire behind it. And as history consistently proves, a church loaded with political power is a recipe for corruption, scriptural abuse, and ultimately division. Sadly the division in this case caused a historical split between two groups God never wanted to be separate. Both were to be founded and rooted as one in His Son. And yet Jesus was now the point of division, just as He had foretold. (See Luke 12:51–53.)

PART II

HOW JESUS COMPLETES
BIBLICAL JUDAISM

Chapter 8

The Nature of God

EVERY FRIDAY IN my sixth-grade class we had show-and-tell, a time when each student got to talk about an object he brought to school that day and explain what it was and why it was significant. While the person was speaking, the object was usually passed around the classroom so everyone could observe the object up close. I was new in the class, having recently changed schools, and so this helped me get to know my classmates better.

One day a boy in my class brought a model airplane and was talking about how he wanted to be a pilot someday as the airplane was sent around the room. I thought this was so cool, and as the airplane finally made its way to me, I took a long time examining the model. While I was doing this, however, the bell rang and the teacher announced that it was time for recess. Without thinking, I instinctively lifted up the top of my desk, placed the model airplane inside, and ran outside to play.

When recess was over and we all returned to the classroom, our teacher asked who had the boy's airplane. I completely forgot what I had done and said nothing. When it remained silent after the teacher asked several more times, she began to get annoyed. Finally she made the whole class search inside our desks. Lo and behold, when I opened up mine, the airplane was right there. It was an innocent mistake, but the teacher accused me of lying and stealing and sent me to the principal's office.

Obviously the teacher was mistaken. The truth was that I was a sensitive young boy who did not practice lying or stealing. But since I had not been in her class long, the teacher had no way of knowing who I really was. In the same way, we can often assume things that are not true about God because we do not fully understand who He is. Before I came to know Jesus, I did not know much about God's character. Likewise, many Jewish people I have known over the years have had little revelation as to who God is, and they sometimes assume things about Him that are contrary to His nature. This is not exclusive to the Jewish people, of course. Regardless of whether you are Jew or Gentile, when you do not know much about God's nature—what He is really like—then you will often see Him with distorted vision or even fail to see Him at all.

This was certainly the case when Jesus walked the earth. The very people who awaited His arrival and who knew hundreds of prophecies about HaMashiach still missed seeing Him when He actually lived before their eyes. Most Jews of Jesus' time were devoted to God's Law, were knowledgeable of His ways and commands, and had His words (the Hebrew Bible) committed to memory, yet many of the Jewish people of Jesus' day still failed to recognize Jesus for who He really was. Of course, many Jews joined in the chorus of hallelujahs and hosannas and cried, "Blessed is He who comes in the name of the Lord!" when Jesus rode triumphantly into Jerusalem (Mark 11:9). But Jewish public opinion against Jesus, influenced by the Pharisees, was also strong enough that only a week later crowds shouted out to Pilate, "Crucify Him!" (Mark 15:13).

How could a people so devoted to their God miss seeing Him up close and personal? I believe one of the primary reasons was because the Jewish people, like many people today, failed to truly understand God's nature. They thought they knew God because they were His chosen people, and yet understood only a limited aspect of who He was rather than seeing the whole of His character.

In the first part of this book we looked at why Judaism and Christianity separated. One of the reasons was the theological challenge Jesus posed for the Jewish people. If He truly was the Messiah, then it meant some of their beliefs about God—that He could not have a son or appear in sinful human flesh, for example—were not accurate. That was certainly a hard pill for the Jews to swallow.

If the Jewish people were to ever recognize the Messiah, they needed to understand how He would fulfill God's commands in the

Torah, as well as the Messianic prophecies found throughout the Tanakh. And in the second half of this book, we will now turn our attention to how Jesus does exactly that—ultimately how He fulfills every element of Judaism. This starts with how Yeshua revealed the true nature of God.

Jesus was a perfect reflection of His Father. He was a mirror image of God. "If you have seen me, you have seen the Father," He said (John 14:9, CEV). Given that, we can conclude that by looking at Jesus' character—who He was when He walked on earth—we will see God's nature revealed in the flesh. And to better understand God, we must understand His nature.

The problem, however, is that people often disconnect the God of the Old Testament from the God of the New Testament. They treat Him as if He were two different Gods with two different natures— one emphasizes holiness, and the other is all about grace. And for most people, including believers, Jesus becomes a separate version of God, different from the God revealed through the Law and the Prophets. Many think that the Old Testament God is holy and judging, while Jesus is loving, kind, and full of grace.

Let's take a look at these two aspects of holiness and grace, then, to see how the Bible actually harmonizes God's nature in the Old and New Testaments, and how Jesus is the fulfillment of both. What we will find is that God's nature is consistent rather than schizophrenic; He is identical in the Tanakh and the B'rit Hadashah. As Hebrews 13:8 says, He is "the same yesterday, and today, and forever."

GOD'S MOST EXALTED ATTRIBUTE

God's most essential attribute is His holiness. The Hebrew word for holy, *qodesh*, means set apart, sacred, separate, or not common.[1] God's supreme holiness is the most crucial aspect of His nature because without this He would not be God but something lower and more common. He is God *because* He is holy and set apart. Numerous times in the Tanakh, the Lord declares that He is holy (Lev. 11:44–45; 19:2; 20:26). Moses found this out when he first met God at the burning bush and the Lord said to Him, "Remove your sandals from off your feet, for the place on which you are standing is holy ground" (Exod. 3:5).

He is the ultimate source of "set-apartness" and is completely distinct from everything else. No one created God, but instead He is the Creator behind everything, as the Bible's first words confirm ("In the beginning God created...," Gen. 1:1). The creation around us may reflect certain attributes of Him—His majesty, splendor, and beauty—and as humans, we may even become like Him in certain ways, but truly no one and nothing is exactly like God. As He declares in Isaiah 45:5, "I am the LORD and there is no other; there is no God besides Me." *This* is why we call Him holy.

To help us understand this, consider Isaiah 45:7, where the Lord says that He is the only One who can "form the light and create darkness; I make peace and create calamity; I, the LORD, do all these things." Simply put, He is the Creator. In the beginning *God* created the heavens and the earth, not anyone else. He alone is the cause that has no cause. Stated another way, God is the first cause, yet He Himself is self-existent. Everything else is created, yet God is uncreated, eternal life and has always been. This is what makes Him so incredibly unique. Truly, as Isaiah 45 states many times, there is none like Him.

God's holiness was and is the foundation of Judaism. In fact, I would venture to say this is the primary attribute of God that is continually emphasized among practicing Jews today. To the Jew, the fact that God is separate, higher, and unlike anything else is the bedrock for why we say in the Shema, "Hear, O Israel: The LORD is our God. The LORD is one!" (Deut. 6:4).

This is for good reason. Did you realize that among all God's countless characteristics, His holiness is the one most emphasized throughout the Bible? It is the only attribute of His nature repeated three times when mentioned. When the prophet Isaiah caught a glimpse of the heavenly throne room and the worship surrounding God, the first thing he heard was these words: "*Holy, holy, holy, is the*

LORD of Hosts; the whole earth is full of His glory" (Isa. 6:3, emphasis added).

Think about it: The angels and heavenly creatures surrounding God's throne could have mentioned countless other qualities of the Lord. But they did not cry, "Worthy, worthy, worthy!" or, "Mighty, mighty, mighty!" They did not echo anything about His love or His justice or His righteousness. No, the first thing declared about God in His presence was, "Qodesh, qodesh, qodesh!"—"Holy, holy, holy!"

That was in the Old Testament; we might expect, then, that the New Testament would highlight a *new* attribute of God, maybe one more reflected in what we saw through Jesus during His time on earth—something like His compassion or healing power or even His salvation of all mankind. In the Book of Revelation, the apostle John goes on a tour of the heavenly throne room just as Isaiah did. John describes the scene with more detail than Isaiah, and yet the very first words he hears in heaven are the exact same as what the prophet heard: "Holy, holy, holy!" In fact, John says the creatures surrounding God's throne *never* stop saying this: "'Holy, holy, holy, Lord God Almighty,' who was, and is, and is to come" (Rev. 4:8). Twenty-four hours a day, seven days a week, those surrounding God's throne declare who He is—His very nature. And the first words spoken about that nature have to do with His holiness.

We could spend an entire chapter on this unique aspect of God's nature, and yet what I want you to note is the continuity in the Old and New Testaments of God's most exalted characteristic. Both the Tanakh and the B'rit Hadashah reveal a God who is consistent within Himself. He does not suffer from a split-personality disorder. He is not holy only in the Old Testament but not holy in the New Testament; He is the same. And yet for some reason, many Jews and Christians alike overlook this when considering who Jesus is.

JESUS' HOLINESS

As God in the flesh, Jesus did not set aside even a fraction of His nature to become human. Philippians 2 describes Jesus as "being in the form of God," yet He "emptied Himself, taking upon Himself the form of a servant, and was made in the likeness of men" (vv. 6–7). This is the profound mystery of Jesus being fully God and fully man—what theologians refer to as His hypostatic union.

Because Jesus possessed the full nature of who God is, He did not leave His holiness in heaven either. He walked the earth with the same "set-apartness" as the Father. We get glimpses of this holiness in moments such as when Jesus encountered a demon-possessed man while teaching in Capernaum's synagogue. As Jesus spoke with unprecedented authority, the man with the unclean spirit "cried out with a loud voice, 'Leave us alone! What have You to do with us, Jesus of Nazareth? Have You come to destroy us? I know who You are—the *Holy* One of God!'" (Luke 4:33–34, emphasis added). The demons inside this man could not help but speak the truth in public because as spiritual beings, they saw Jesus in His true nature—holy.

Later in Jesus' life this holiness was just as evident when soldiers came to arrest Him in the Garden of Gethsemane. Upon their arrival, Jesus asked whom they sought. When they said they were looking for Jesus of Nazareth, most Scripture translations say that He responded with three simple words: "I am He." "When He said, 'I am He,' they drew back and fell to the ground" (John 18:6). The more accurate translation might be that Jesus spoke aloud the same name He revealed to Moses at the burning bush hundreds of years before: "I AM WHO I AM" (Exod. 3:14). Jesus did not just respond casually to the soldiers with, "Yep, that's Me, guys. I'm the One you're looking for." He spoke aloud His name, Yahweh, which the Jewish law reveres as so holy it should not be spoken or written. This is why today in Jewish prayer books the Lord is referred to as Adonai instead of by His name. The power behind God's holy name made all flesh present in the garden that night fall to the ground before Him.

Isn't it profound, then, that Jesus invites us to talk and commune with this same holy God? When Jesus taught His disciples to pray, He immediately drew their attention to God's holiness. The Lord's Prayer begins with, "Our Father, who is in heaven, hallowed be Your name" (Luke 11:2). The word *hallowed* is simply an older English word to describe something holy, set apart, and worthy of the utmost honor. God's very name is holy.

God's holiness is why He is God. In the Old Testament He chose to reveal Himself in spirit to a select few people, and in the New Testament He chose to reveal Himself in flesh to the world in the form of Jesus Christ. It is crucial, then, for us to consider that Jesus, because He *is* the essence of God's holiness, is worthy of the same honor.

GOD'S GRACE THROUGH MOSES

For many believers today, holiness is not necessarily the first thing they think of when they think of Jesus. Instead, they associate countless other attributes of God's nature—His love, kindness, compassion, power, or authority. These words seem more "New Testament" than terms such as *holiness, righteousness,* or *justice.* And perhaps no word carries a stronger association to the New Testament than the word *grace.*

What I find fascinating is that many people struggle to connect the God of the Old Testament with grace, just as many people struggle to connect the Jesus of the New Testament with holiness. Again, God is unchanging. Regarding His relationship with man, He is the same "yesterday, and today, and forever" (Heb. 13:8). That means the Old Testament God was just as filled with grace as Jesus was on the cross.

Think about it: If Jesus was the image of God, and if Jesus showed the utmost grace by reconnecting us to God even though we do not deserve it, then how is it possible for God to be any different in the Old Testament? How could He be any "less" filled with grace? He cannot! But because so many people struggle to see this and instead view God as only being wrathful in the Old Testament, let's take a further look at how we can find such grace running throughout the Old Testament.

When God called Moses to lead His people out of Egypt, the Lord knew it would not be an easy assignment. He knew Moses' patience and grace would be stretched to the limit, just as His own were at times with those He called a "stiff-necked people" (Exod. 32:9). While Moses met with God on Mount Sinai and received the Law, the Jewish people grew restless and molded a golden calf to worship. God grew so frustrated with them that He told Moses, "Now therefore let Me alone, so that My wrath may burn against them and I may destroy them. And I will make of you a great nation" (v. 10).

It would have been so easy for Moses to go along with God; these were indeed a difficult people who at times infuriated Moses. But instead he stepped in and reminded God not only of His promises to Abraham, Isaac, and Jacob but also that Egypt would think wrongly of the Lord if He killed the Jewish people only a short time after liberating them. After Moses argued his case, Scripture records in matter-of-fact terms a fascinating turn of events: "Then the LORD relented of the harm which He said He would do to His people" (Exod. 32:14). Theologians and apologists have debated this verse and its implications for generations, pondering the question of if we can actually change an omniscient God's mind. I have no intention of arguing that case here, but I do want you to notice how these events created an opportunity for God's grace to be on full display.

When Moses pleaded for the Lord to not destroy the Jewish people, Moses was serving as Israel's intercessor—he stood between them and God's wrath, asking God to show mercy by not wiping them out. Did they deserve to die? Most certainly, for not only had they broken one of the Ten Commandments and worshipped an idol, but also their hearts had turned against God. Under the Law, their sin deserved a punishment. And yet what prevented this punishment? God's grace—His undeserved, unmerited favor!

God knew His people were not faithful and would turn to idolatry because He knew their hearts. By keeping Moses up on Mount Sinai for as long as He did, He knew the Israelites would eventually act upon what was in their hearts. So the Lord knew the longer He took with Moses, the more likely the Jewish people would fall into sin. But I would argue that He did not linger because He was chomping at the bit for an opportunity to bring judgment, but that

He was waiting for an opportunity to reveal His grace. God's law and grace are not mutually exclusive but go hand in hand, as we will examine more in the next chapter.

For now, however, I want you to recognize how powerfully Jesus is revealed through Moses in this passage. Moses interceded for a people deserving death, and the outcome was a revealing of God's grace. More than fifteen hundred years later Jesus interceded on the cross for a human race deserving death and eternal punishment, and the outcome was the greatest example of grace ever given. Even though Moses had done nothing wrong amid a people who mocked him and judged him, Moses stood before God asking for forgiveness on their behalf and offering his own life in exchange for theirs. "Yet now, if You will," Moses prayed, "forgive their sin, but if not, I pray, blot me out of Your book which You have written" (Exod. 32:32).

In an even greater way, Jesus lived among a people who mocked, hated, beat, and ultimately killed Him, and yet He asked God to forgive them and offered His own life on their behalf. Jesus was the only sinless man to ever live; He was absolutely the last man on earth who deserved to die for breaking God's Law. So when He bore our sins on the cross, He revealed the very nature of God—that He *is* grace.

Yet we must understand that God did not suddenly become filled with grace while Jesus was on earth, as if He unexpectedly changed His character from a mean, judging God of the Old Testament to a kinder, gentler deity in the New Testament. No, just as with Moses at Sinai, God established a means to reveal His undeserved favor upon a people—sinful humanity—who actually deserved to die. Through Jesus He took the punishment we all deserved and exchanged it for the opportunity for eternal life with Him. That is truly *amazing* grace!

Jesus fulfilled the Law yet faced its punishment *so that* God's grace could be revealed. Isn't it fascinating that we can see this on display as far back as Moses, who was an archetype of Jesus? Moses was willing to take the blame for his people, yet God used his willingness— and their breaking of the Law—as a means to extend grace rather than justice. Moses, therefore, was a precursor to a greater grace, shown through Jesus. As one apologist observed, "God listened to Moses because God would listen to Jesus."[2] God allowed Moses to intercede for His people, Israel, because He knew one day His own Son would intercede for all people. And in both situations mercy triumphed over justice (James 2:13). Why? Because God's very nature is to give grace where it is not deserved. Hallelujah!

IN THE PRESENCE OF GRACE

It is impossible for us to receive a true revelation of who God is without encountering His grace. When we stand before a holy God—the God who is the same in both the Old and New Testaments, whom creatures ceaselessly laud as holy in His throne room—we also stand before a God full of grace. The truth is that we are human and He is God; therefore our mere presence before Him requires grace. He is holy, and we are not, and any combination of the two parties merits grace on His behalf.

Moses discovered this truth shortly after His exchange with God on Mount Sinai. After descending the mountain, he eventually set up a tent among the people where "the LORD spoke to Moses face to face, just as a man speaks to his friend" (Exod. 33:11). Talk about being in God's presence! In fact, Moses grew so accustomed to being in the Lord's presence that he concluded the Jewish people would be hopeless and helpless if they were without it. "If Your Presence does not go with us, do not bring us up from here," Moses stated (v. 15). God reassured Moses that He would lead him and His people, and He even promised to reveal more of Himself to Moses at the prophet's request. But it is *how* God revealed Himself that we need to take note of.

Up to that point in time we know that God and Moses had had many lengthy discussions on the details of the Law. Remember, Moses had been up on Mount Sinai with the Lord for forty days and nights, during which the Lord had given him the entire Law—both the Ten Commandments and specific guidelines for how the Israelites were to live (Exod. 24:18). God had also given Moses instructions for building the tabernacle, the altar, and the ark of the covenant, as well as many other things. Much of the Law consisted of the conditions for blessings and curses. So we might assume that when Moses asked to see more of God—"Show me Your glory" (Exod. 33:18)—the Lord would come as the great judge, the great teacher, or the great explainer of these commandments He had given. But did the Lord come as a harsh, black-and-white lawgiver? Did He begin to explain more about the technicalities behind His commands? No, Exodus 34 records a very different scene than what we might expect:

> Then the LORD came down in the cloud and stood there with him and proclaimed his name, the LORD. And he passed in front of Moses, proclaiming, "The LORD, the LORD, the compassionate and gracious God, slow to anger, abounding in love and faithfulness, maintaining love to thousands, and forgiving wickedness, rebellion and sin. Yet he does not leave the guilty unpunished; he punishes the children and their children for the sin of the parents to the third and fourth generation."
>
> —EXODUS 34:5–7, NIV

God proclaimed His own nature and character to Moses, and the very first way He described Himself was as "compassionate and gracious." God's compassion flows out of His grace. In fact, the Hebrew word that is translated in English as "compassion" is *rachum*. The root word actually means "womb," so *rachum* is a word picture describing the same compassion and love a mother would have toward her baby. It is emotional and passionate—the complete opposite of heartless and unfeeling. So when the Lord revealed more of His nature to Moses, this grace-filled, merciful compassion is what He presented first.

The Lord had rachum for Moses because that is in His nature. In the same way, He had rachum for His people, Israel, despite their disobedience, stubbornness, hard-heartedness, grumbling, and frequent opposition toward their God. The Lord is full of grace. He offers love and compassion where none is deserved. He shows mercy to those who should rightfully be punished. And like a mother with her child, He loves with a fervent, passionate, embracing love.

Generations later David would attest to the same attributes of God in the psalms he wrote. David knew God as a God of grace and love because of their unique relationship. While Moses was a friend of the Lord who met with Him face to face, God called David "a man after My own heart" (Acts 13:22). Because of their intimate relationship, David could write from experience, "You, O Lord, are a God full of compassion and gracious, slow to anger, and abundant in mercy and truth" (Ps. 86:15). In one of my favorite psalms, Psalm 18, he wrote, "Your gentleness has made me great" (v. 35). David certainly knew the holiness of God that we find featured prominently throughout the Old Testament, yet he also knew God's grace just as well.

Whether it is in the writings of Moses, David, Isaiah, or the apostle John, we find the same truth echoed throughout the Bible: God is one. The Shema holds such power for Jews because it is a touchstone for understanding God's nature. He is not inconsistent. His holiness is not in contrast to His grace. His love does not nullify His justice or even His right to judge. He is the same God throughout the entire Bible. The God who appeared in fire atop Mount Sinai is the same God who appeared in flesh through Jesus, healing those who followed Him throughout Galilee, Judea, and beyond.

The more we grasp this revelation and truly see God for who He is, the more we will also see a unity in His Word like never before. When that happens, the Old Testament begins to fit together with the New Testament like a hand in a glove. As you and I continue to seek His face and draw near to Him, He will continue by the Holy Spirit to reveal His nature more and more to us.

CHAPTER 9

LAW AND GRACE

I CANNOT IMAGINE WHAT it was like for Moses to stand with the Lord atop Mount Sinai and have his senses overwhelmed as God literally passed by him. In the previous chapter, we looked at how the Lord honored Moses' request to see His glory. Let's revisit that scene once more:

> Then Moses said, "I pray, show me Your glory."... Then the LORD descended in the cloud, and stood with him there, and proclaimed the name of the LORD. The LORD passed by before him, and proclaimed, "The LORD, the LORD God, merciful and gracious, slow to anger, and abounding in goodness and truth, keeping mercy for thousands, forgiving iniquity and transgression and sin, but who will by no means clear the guilty, visiting the iniquity of fathers on the children and on the children's children, to the third and the fourth generation."
> —EXODUS 33:18; 34:5–7

When you think of the first few sentences of this passage, the scene gets a bit tricky. How did God come down and stand with Moses yet also pass by him? Furthermore, what does it really mean that the Lord "proclaimed the name of the LORD" (v. 5)? Was God simply saying His own name and describing Himself to Moses, or was there something else involved in Him showing His glory to Moses? To complicate matters, let's not forget that what Moses experienced was simply the back of God, for the Lord had previously told him, "While My glory passes by, I will put you in a cleft of the rock and will cover you with My hand while I pass by. Then I will take away My hand, and you will see My back, but My face may not be seen" (Exod. 33:22–23). If you feel a little confused, know that you are not alone. It is very likely that what actually happened that day atop Mount Sinai is beyond our comprehension.

As difficult as it may be for us to visualize the scene described in Exodus 34, it is important for us to at least recognize that God revealed many aspects of His nature to Moses during this encounter. Jewish people call these the Thirteen Attributes of God and have historically paid special interest to each aspect God mentioned in Exodus 34:6–7. These thirteen attributes, according to Jewish study, include such traits as His sovereignty, compassion, forgiveness, and overflowing loving-kindness.

In the last chapter, we spent some time examining two of these aspects: His holiness and His grace. We also looked into the importance of God first revealing Himself as a compassionate, loving God rather than just a harsh lawgiver. Notice, however, that although God spoke of His "mercy for thousands" that forgives and is "abounding in goodness," He still mentioned that He does not "clear the guilty" but allows them to reap the consequences of their sin (Exod. 34:6–7). Why would the Lord end His revelation to Moses on such an ominous note? Why would He include that in the mix of revealing His glory when all the other attributes seem so much more praiseworthy? I believe the answer to these questions is crucial for us to understand as we attempt to grasp how God's Law and His grace coexist.

As we discussed earlier in this book, many people are confused about God because they see Him as being mostly focused on judgment and wrath in the Old Testament, but then suddenly putting on His happy face in the New Testament and becoming a nice deity who is full of love, grace, and mercy. I hope you have already discovered this to be false and that you can attest to the fact that God is the same God in both the Old and New Testaments. Jesus came to earth as the living example of what God looks like, and He is both holy and full of grace.

I meet countless believers, however, who walk out their faith as if the holiness of the Law and the grace of Jesus Christ are in opposition and God must be one or the other. They view the Old Testament commandments of God—the Law—as incompatible and mutually exclusive with the New Testament theme of grace found through Yeshua HaMashiach. As a result, many people ultimately experience a core misunderstanding of God. They see Him as only a God of law in the Tanakh and only a God of grace in the B'rit Hadashah. This is not the case, as we will soon see.

Unfortunately Christian history has not always helped to clear up this misunderstanding. In chapter 5 we looked at how anti-Semitism crept into Christianity and began to tear the church further away from its Jewish roots. This shifted the church's theology, including how believers viewed the Law. Whereas the early Jewish church understood the Law to be God's commands in order to bring about blessing, the growing Gentile church began to see the Law as a burden to be cast off. Because Jesus often rebuked the Pharisees and religious leaders for following the Law yet forgetting its intent, the Gentile believers of the first few centuries began to believe that the Law was obsolete and nullified. These believers unknowingly tossed out the baby with the bathwater, as they were unable to separate the Law's true purpose from its misuse.

Such views of the Law and its contrast to the grace of Jesus have continued throughout church history. One example of this can be found in the area of Bible translation, which has a tremendous impact on shifting church theology. In 1611 the King James Version of the Bible was completed, making available a version that translated the original texts into the English language while also conforming to the Church of England's doctrines and culture. Yet in certain passages wrong theology affected the King James Version's translation— and therefore how people read Scripture.

For example, John 1:16–17 was translated in the King James Version as: "And of his fullness have all we received, and grace for grace. For the law was given by Moses, *but* grace and truth came by Jesus Christ." Notice in verse 17 how the word *but* is italicized, just as it has been in the King James Version's printed version for centuries. By italicizing the word *but*, the translators indicated that it was added and is not in the ancient manuscripts on which their translation was based. They added the comparative word because they thought it would make the meaning of the verse clearer, but, in fact, because of faulty theology the translators actually misunderstood the verse completely. Let me explain.

Imagine that your boss called you into his office and said, "You did a really good job on this, *but*..." Do you think what he will say next will be another compliment? Of course not! The nature of the word *but* is that it introduces something that will contrast with what has preceded it. For example, if somebody says to you, "Your dress looks really nice, *but*...," do you think the person is now going to say how great your shoes look? Or if a mechanic says to you, "Your car runs great, *but*...," is it likely he will now tell you what great mileage it gets? No, they are setting you up first with something positive to then point out something that is not so good. *But* sets up opposites; you are heading one direction, and you then must shift to another direction.

With this in mind, let's look at these verses again as translated by the King James translators. "And of his fullness have all we received, and grace for grace. For the law was given by Moses, *but* grace and truth came by Jesus Christ" (John 1:16–17). Notice how the King James Version sets up a contrast—dare I say an opposition—between the Law given by Moses and the grace revealed through Jesus. The translation makes it sound as if the Law of the Lord is the opposite of the grace of God. Sadly this anti-Law mentality parallels the anti-Jewish theology of the time in which the King James Version was created. The translators, with a bias against the "Christ-killing" Jews, were pitting Jesus against the Law. Unfortunately the general church adopted this mind-set, and the King James Version has shaped our theology for generations since.

I am not trying to pick on the King James Version. Every Bible translation has limitations and cultural influences, and every version contains errors. That is to be expected when trying to translate ancient documents written across a time span of more than two thousand years. But this case exemplifies how the wrong theology—formed even with just the addition of a three-letter word in a Bible verse—can influence the church's beliefs and even its view of the Lord. God's Law is not contrary to His grace. I believe John's original intention in writing those verses was to express that the Law itself is a *manifestation* of God's grace. The underlying purpose of the Law is to reveal the amazing grace of the Lord.

"Grace Upon Grace"

Notice the unusual phrase John used in the first verse I quoted. In referring to Jesus, he wrote: "We have all received from His fullness grace upon grace" (John 1:16). What does "grace upon grace" mean? It seems strange to mention grace twice, yet John's unique phrase points to the layered aspect of God's grace revealed over time. The first grace John refers to is the Law—the original commandments and way of living meant to bless Israel. How was the Law itself a form of grace? Because it was actually a preliminary manifestation of God's greater grace, shown more fully through Jesus. Again, let me explain.

At the time of Moses, Israel lived in a barbaric world. There was no "law of the land," no police, no jurisdiction, and no fair system of justice. When societies and people groups are lawless, then there is nothing to keep people restrained. For example, if someone stole my camel back then, nothing would have prevented me from retaliating by going to where the culprit lived, murdering his wife and kids, and burning down his house.

Through God's Law, however, a new standard was established: an eye for an eye, and a tooth for a tooth. In other words, the punishment needed to fit the crime. I no longer had the right to go burn down someone's house just for stealing my camel. The Law, then, lifted Israel out of the base standards of that period in history. These were not the commandments of a harsh lawgiver but rather the guidance of a gracious God, elevating His children above the barbarian societies of their day to live in a kingdom governed by laws of grace. This is why Moses said to Israel:

See, I have taught you statutes and judgments, just as the LORD my God commanded me, that you should do so in the land where you are entering to possess it. Therefore, keep and do them, for this is your wisdom and your understanding in the sight of the nations which shall hear all these statutes, and say, "Surely this great nation is a wise and understanding people." For what nation is there so great, who has a god so near to it as the LORD our God is in all things whenever we call on Him? *And what nation is there so great that has statutes and judgments so righteous as all this law,* which I am setting before you today?

—DEUTERONOMY 4:5–8, EMPHASIS ADDED

Too often we think of the Law as merely oppressive and burdensome. But God's purposes for the Law were full of grace. He wanted His people to enjoy the unmerited fruits of righteousness by living according to a higher, godly standard. By His grace the people of Israel could live differently and fulfill His original covenant with Abraham that through them "all families of the earth [would] be blessed" (Gen. 12:3).

As we know, however, the children of Israel began to live not under God's grace but by their own religious performance. Over generations the nation's religious leaders began to pile customs, traditions, and new laws upon what God originally established, and the result was that the Law became a burden.

This was how it was when Jesus came and why He opposed the religious leaders so fiercely. He came to set people free from the burden and punishment of the Law as well as the burden of tradition that Israel's religious leaders had attached to it. Jesus came to extend a greater grace to people, and this is the second grace John mentions when he uses the phrase "grace upon grace" (John 1:16). The people of God could see God's grace in the original Law. But when Jesus came, they received an entirely new and more complete picture of God's grace.

The Book of Hebrews tells us, "In the past God spoke to our

ancestors through the prophets at many times and in various ways, but in these last days he has spoken to us by his Son, whom he appointed heir of all things, and through whom also he made the universe" (1:1–2, NIV). The Law was like a beam of the sun's rays, but Jesus is the full sun shining. When Jesus came to earth, grace could be understood, seen, and received in a far greater way.

RAISING THE BAR

Jesus did not just reveal God's grace; He took it to another level. Before Yeshua came, Israel had already been pulled out of the barbaric standards of the time. Through the Law of Moses, God elevated them into a new system of justice that reflected God's righteousness and His grace. When Jesus began to teach, however, He revealed God's ultimate plan, one that shook up the entire system.

> You have heard that it was said by the ancients, "You shall not murder," and "Whoever murders shall be in danger of the judgment." But I say to you that whoever is angry with his brother without a cause shall be in danger of the judgment....
>
> You have heard that it was said by the ancients, "You shall not commit adultery." But I say to you that whoever looks on a woman to lust after her has committed adultery with her already in his heart....
>
> It was said, "Whoever divorces his wife, let him give her a certificate of divorce." But I say to you that whoever divorces his wife, except for marital unfaithfulness, causes her to commit adultery. And whoever marries her who is divorced commits adultery....
>
> You have heard that it was said, "An eye for an eye, and a tooth for a tooth." But I say to you, do not resist an evil person. But whoever strikes you on your right cheek, turn to him the other as well. And if anyone sues you in a court of law and takes away your tunic, let him have your cloak also. And whoever compels you to go a mile, go with him two....

> You have heard that it was said, "You shall love your
> neighbor and hate your enemy." But I say to you, love your
> enemies, bless those who curse you, do good to those who
> hate you, and pray for those who spitefully use you and
> persecute you, that you may be sons of your Father who is
> in heaven.
>
> —MATTHEW 5:21–22, 27–28, 31–32, 38–41, 43–45

How could Jesus dare to say such things? What was He doing?
To His Jewish listeners, who knew the Law well enough to recognize every Torah verse He quoted, it certainly must have sounded as
if Jesus was changing God's Law. God had commanded them, "You
shall not add to the word which I am commanding you, nor shall you
take anything from it, so that you may keep the commandments of
the LORD your God which I command you" (Deut. 4:2). Yet here was
Jesus doing just that! You can imagine how much of a struggle this
was for both those listening and, in particular, the Jewish religious
leaders. So why would Jesus do this so early in His ministry?

To answer this, we need to pay attention to the context of what
Jesus said. Before He launched into a series of "You have heard that
it was said…" expressions of the "greater law," He made a statement
that we have referred to throughout this book but that is critical in
order for us to understand how He is the fulfillment of Judaism and
the Law. In Matthew 5:17, just a few verses before His first "update"
of the Law, Jesus said:

> Do not think that I have come to abolish the Law or the
> Prophets. I have not come to abolish, but to fulfill. For truly
> I say to you, until heaven and earth pass away, not one dot
> or one mark will pass from the law until all be fulfilled.
> Whoever, therefore, breaks one of the least of these com-
> mandments and teaches others to do likewise shall be called
> the least in the kingdom of heaven. But whoever does and
> teaches them shall be called great in the kingdom of heaven.
> For I say to you that unless your righteousness exceeds the

righteousness of the scribes and Pharisees, you will in no
way enter the kingdom of heaven.
                                               —MATTHEW 5:17–20

Not only did Jesus come to fulfill the Law, but He came to fulfill
it to the highest degree—so much so that every "dot" and "mark" of
the Law would be completed. In teaching His Jewish disciples, Jesus
first elevated the Law, and then from this position, in this context,
He launched into what is a higher version of the Law. What version
is this? The "grace upon grace" version!

Essentially Jesus was saying, "The Law says the standard is 'an eye
for an eye, and a tooth for a tooth'; now let Me raise the bar and
command you to extend even more grace to each other—so much
that you're willing to turn the other cheek even when you're not at
fault, or to give away everything you own to the person who's wrong-
fully trying to take it all from you."

It was difficult to adhere to every command of the Law before;
was Jesus now making it impossible for His disciples to follow it?
Without grace, yes—although the Law had already done that. What
Jesus was revealing was the way of His kingdom. This kingdom was
full of grace—so much that when someone did evil against you, the
response now called for forgiveness instead of bitterness, love instead
of hatred, and mercy instead of judgment. Jesus was introducing a
new standard both of the Law *and* of His grace. Jesus was calling
His followers to a higher level than the Mosaic Law; He was calling
them to a mountain even higher than Mount Sinai. Moses had asked
God to reveal more of Himself to him on Sinai, and here was Jesus
revealing more of Himself to His followers atop another mountain.

What is fascinating is that Jesus gave us the choice as to which law
we would hold others to: the Law of Moses or the law of higher grace.
He gave us free will. If we want to, we can keep someone bound to
the Mosaic Law. We can continue on with an "eye for an eye" system.
But Jesus reminded His followers, "In everything, do to others what
you would have them do to you, for this sums up the Law and the
Prophets" (Matt. 7:12, NIV).

That posed a problem because the truth is that we rarely want an equal return. Too often we live by a double standard. When we do something wrong, we want forgiveness, but when someone does us wrong, our natural, human tendency is to hold the person to the Law. We want him to be held accountable for what he did, or we may even want vengeance. This reveals our double nature not just with each other but also with God. How often do we want God to extend forgiveness and grace to us, yet when our brother or sister does us wrong, we want judgment?

Jesus' new system created a radical new challenge. Would we be willing to forgive those who hurt us? Stated another way, would we be willing to release our offenders from the Law under which they deserved to be judged? Jesus said whatever measurement we choose to use on others, that is the same one we will be measured by:

> Judge not, and you shall not be judged. Condemn not, and you will not be condemned. Forgive, and you shall be forgiven. Give, and it will be given to you: Good measure, pressed down, shaken together, and running over will men give unto you. For with the measure you use, it will be measured unto you.
>
> —LUKE 6:37–38

Here is the wonderful news: if we are willing to live by Jesus' new kingdom standards, then we are actually walking in "grace upon grace" and reflecting the very nature of God Himself. The more we do this, the more Christlike we become. What a concept! We who deserve punishment under the Law can now be the righteousness of God on the earth.

In the Old Testament, God gave His people, Israel, commands to live as a holy nation that would reflect His nature to the rest of the world. Yet in order to live holy, they needed His grace. The Law itself only emphasized their need for His grace. And His grace completed the Law. Yet who was the fulfillment of the Law *and* the living expression of God's grace? Jesus! Yeshua is the ultimate fulfillment of both the Law and grace. And this revelation is key to both Jews and Christians recognizing how Jesus completes the Old Testament, with its theme of the Law, *and* the New Testament, with its emphasis on grace.

God revealed a greater measurement of His grace *and* a higher purpose of the Law when He sent Jesus. He has called us out of living *under* the Law to a life of living *above* it through the grace of Jesus Christ. When Jesus hung on the cross, He looked upon those who spit on Him, pulled out His beard, mocked Him, and pierced Him, and He said, "Father, forgive them, for they know not what they do" (Luke 23:34). Are you willing to offer the same amazing grace, the same radical forgiveness, and the same divine love to those who do wrong to you? If so, know that you are walking in the perfect compatibility found in God's kingdom between law and grace.

CHAPTER 10

THE PURPOSE OF THE LAW

Y EARS AGO I went to a local department store where a salesman had set up a display showing the incredible ShamWow cloths that had just come out and were quickly becoming a TV infomercial sensation. I was with my daughter, who was seven years old at the time, and we were both *wowed* by the demonstration. The salesman spilled a pitcher of water on a display counter that he had set up, and with one sweep of the blue ShamWow cloth he completely absorbed all the water from the countertop. Amazing! Then, after wringing out all the water, he stuck the rag in the pitcher of water, pulled out the ShamWow, rang it out once again, and showed how the cloth had absorbed a quarter of the pitcher of water. Sensational!

I was convinced and bought the ShamWow package of eight cloths for $19.95. In the car on the way home, my daughter said she wanted me to become a ShamWow salesman—that's how excited we both were about our purchase. We couldn't wait to get home and show my wife.

Her response, however, was not what we expected. As we demonstrated the ShamWow's amazing capabilities and did our best to mimic the salesman's display, my wife began to chuckle.

"So what's the point?" she asked.

"Huh?" I said in bewilderment. "We just showed you all the cool things it can do. What do you mean, what's the point?" How could she *not* be wowed by the ShamWow?

My wife went into our washroom, pulled out some of the cheap rags she usually used to clean, and showed us how they could do exactly the same thing. My heart sank. If an old rag worth pennies was just as "amazing," then why had I spent so much on these silly cloths? If the ShamWow wasn't as special as what it was hyped up to be, then what was the point?

Many people ask the same question when it comes to the Law in the context of God's covenants. If God knew His people would be unable to follow the Law, then what was the point of it? Why were His commands so specific, and why did they demand so much from the Jewish people? And why were there so many laws? I often hear people confused about the underlying purpose of God's commandments to Israel. In their lack of understanding, many people disregard the importance of the Law. And in light of Jesus they often minimize its role, making it irrelevant both today and in the past.

But the Law was—and still is—anything but irrelevant. Remember, Jesus said He came to *fulfill* the Law, not abolish it (Matt. 5:17). In fact, He pointed to the fact that "until heaven and earth pass away, not one dot or one mark will pass from the law until all be fulfilled" (v. 18). That means not only did the Law have purpose in the Old Testament times, but it continues to have a purpose today and will continue to have one until the end of time. With that profound thought in mind, let's dig a little deeper into what exactly was and is the purpose of the Law. I believe that as we do that, you will begin to receive a greater revelation of God's ultimate plan, which is fulfilled in Jesus Christ.

As we begin, realize that one of the profound mysteries of the Law is its dual nature. From the time God first gave His commandments to Moses, the Law immediately took on a twofold purpose: an original purpose, as expressed in the time of Moses; and an eternal purpose, as expressed through Jesus Christ for all time. So as we examine at least five major purposes of the Law in this chapter, we would benefit from keeping this dual nature of the Law in mind, as it will help us discover not only *how* God used the Law (its function) but also *why* He established it in the first place (its purpose).

PURPOSE 1: TO REVEAL GOD'S NATURE

The giving of the Law was a cosmic climax. When God appeared before Israel at Mount Sinai, He came in awesome, terrifying glory.

Fire. Smoke. Dark clouds. Thunder. Lightning. Ear-splitting trum-
pets. Even the mountain itself shook violently—and this was all just
a precursor to the Lord arriving on top of Mount Sinai to meet pri-
vately with Moses.

This was the first time in history the God of all creation cosmically
and visibly revealed Himself to a mass of people. In fact, more than a
million people simultaneously saw Him. The Hebrew Bible records
that "all the people witnessed the thunder and the lightning and the
sound of the trumpet and the mountain smoking; and when the people saw it, they trembled and stood at a distance" (Exod. 20:18). Had
any of us been there, I am sure we would have done the same thing.
When God physically reveals Himself, it can be terrifying.

But God's revelation to the Jewish people was not just a one-time
physical event. God revealed Himself more by giving His people the
Law, which was an expression of His very nature. The Lord did not
give the Jewish people just regulations, rituals, and commandments,
but instead a picture of who He is.

Many of us today read the passages of the Torah that convey the
Law and feel overwhelmed by its extraordinary details.* If that is all
we get out of our reading, however, then unfortunately we are miss-
ing the point. Throughout the Law we find multiple revelations of
God's heart, not just dry regulations. We get a clearer picture of who
God is the more we examine the "details" of the Law and even what
is behind those details. Within the Law, God revealed His holiness,
His love, His forgiveness, His justice, His generosity to both Jew and
Gentile, and His compassion and concern for the poor and oppressed.
The Law was not just hard rules but part of God's self-revelation.

Like God, the Law was also multidimensional. Part of the Law
was ceremonial, with instructions on the elements that set apart the
Israelites from other nations—distinctions such as circumcision, eating kosher, or observing Shabbat. Part of the Law was sacrificial, giving detailed procedures and directions on how the temple ordinances

---

* The Torah contains more than just the Law; it is "the book" (five books in one) of Moses' teachings. In fact, the Law is not mentioned until the Book of Exodus.

were to be administered. Another part of the law was civil and dealt with issues of justice and land distribution while Israel inhabited its land. Still another part was moral or ethical and brought order to society and relationships. Through all these different facets of the Law we can find aspects of God's multidimensional nature expressed.

We must remember that God first drew the Israelites into relationship with Him, and out of that relationship came the Law. The Lord did not immediately throw a bunch of rules and regulations at His people and say, "Good luck with all that!" He first drew them to Himself by showing His compassion, mercy, provision, safety, love, forgiveness, and grace when He delivered them out of slavery and bondage. The Law was given as an expression of His relationship with His people. For example, He showed them He was holy at Mount Sinai, and then that holiness was on full display through the Law He gave them. In short, the Law revealed more of God.

When Jesus came, He took this revelation to a whole new level. Because of Jesus people could now see God up close and personal. Yeshua gave us a fuller image of God and revealed to us more of His nature. "He who has seen Me has seen the Father," Jesus said (John 14:9). Conversely, He told the Jews of His time, "If you had known Me, you would have known My Father also" (v. 7). But to those who believed in Him, He continued: "From now on you do know Him and have seen Him" (v. 7). By looking at the man named Jesus who was living, breathing, and speaking before them, they *had* seen God in the flesh. So Jesus could only say these things because He had fulfilled one of the purposes of the Law: to reveal God.

PURPOSE 2: TO SET APART GOD'S PEOPLE

The Law of Moses set apart Israel from all other nations. As we mentioned in the previous chapter, Israel lived in a barbaric world where lawlessness ruled the day. God's Law lifted them out of that chaos and disorder and distinguished them from every other culture and people group. God had declared to the Jewish people, "You shall be holy unto Me; for I the LORD am holy and have separated you from other peoples, that you should be Mine" (Lev. 20:26).

What actually set the Israelites apart? For starters, they were instrumental in introducing monotheism to the world.[1] Worshipping only one god seemed foolish to most of those around them, yet this was God's command: "You shall have no other gods before Me" (Exod. 20:3). The fact that this was God's *very first* command to His people highlights just how much it would set them apart from the rest of the world—and indeed, their tendency to break this command more than any other makes it obvious that monotheism was an anomaly.

In addition, God set apart His people through circumcision, which was unheard of before. The Lord placed a physical mark upon His people that distinguished them as "called out" and symbolized both His intimate covenant with them and their "circumcised" hearts devoted to Him (Deut. 10:16).

God set apart Israel through its diet, introducing a kosher way of eating unlike other nations. Though other cultures could indulge in whatever they wanted, God held a higher standard for His holy people—a standard that even doctors and nutritionists to this day swear leads to a healthier, longer life.

From what the Jews wore to whom they married to how they governed people, the Law set apart Israel from the sinful, godless, lawless peoples surrounding them. As the Torah declared, "For you are a holy people to the LORD your God. The LORD your God has chosen you to be His special people, treasured above all peoples who are on the face of the earth" (Deut. 7:6).

No other nation would be like Israel, and that is how God designed it, so that all people would see Him whenever they looked at the Jewish people. The Law would set them apart and make them great, as Moses declared: "For what nation is there so great, who has a god so near to it as the LORD our God is in all things whenever we call on Him? And what nation is there so great that has statutes and judgments so righteous as all this law, which I am setting before you today?" (Deut. 4:7–8).

In the same way, Jesus sets His followers apart from the standards of this world. We are now called to live holy by His grace. Whereas the Jews could not live up to God's standards of holiness (which we'll discuss shortly), we now are declared holy *in Jesus*, who fulfilled the Law for us. The Law simultaneously reveals our shortcomings while accentuating God's grace by declaring us righteous even though, when left on our own, we are anything but that. Yeshua, then, fulfills the Law's purpose by setting a people apart unto God the Father in Himself. And He is now calling to Himself anyone who will respond and obey.

Purpose 3: To Instruct and Guide

Learning elementary Hebrew was not easy for me. As a young man, I did not learn the language by osmosis; just because I hung around others who spoke Hebrew did not mean I would automatically pick it up. I had to study and work hard just to acquire the basics, and equally important I needed someone to teach me. As an adult, I hired a tutor who moved to the United States from Israel, and I went to her home for an hour lesson twice a week. For most people, the best way to learn a language—or most things, for that matter—is to have someone or something to instruct you, just as I did.

God knew that for Israel to be a holy people, they would need instructions and guidance. This was one of the fundamental reasons He gave them the Law, which served as a "guidebook" for life. The entire Torah is a holy teaching document that shows how God relates to mankind and how He desires that we relate to Him. But this was not just a primer. The Law defined things that before had remained undefined and elaborated on details where previously things had been vague. It established a moral code and set healthy boundaries for relationships and communication. It offered structure for everything from business dealings to eating habits, and it set a framework for the Jewish society.

The nations took notice of God's blessing upon the Jewish people, and during its times of faithfulness and obedience to the Lord, Israel was the envy among nations. Yet this was always contingent upon how closely the people followed the Law both in action and with their hearts.

Jesus' harshest dealings were with those who claimed to follow the Law to a tee but had lost sight of its underlying purpose, which was to reflect God's nature and heart. The religious leaders of His time took pride in their personal adherence to the Law, and yet Jesus routinely rebuked them for burdening people with commands God never gave. "These people draw near to Me with their mouth, and honor Me with their lips, but their heart is far from Me," Jesus said. "In vain they do worship Me, teaching as doctrines the precepts of men" (Matt. 15:8–9). The Lord was actually quoting Isaiah 29:13 when He said this, which meant that things had not changed much from the prophet's time. Too often we can rest on our spiritual laurels, yet God gave the Law to teach us how to rely on Him for our daily needs of every kind. This is why the Lord originally told the Jewish people:

> You must carefully keep all the commandments that I am commanding you today, so that you may live, and multiply, and go in and possess the land which the LORD swore to your fathers. You must remember that the LORD your God led you all the way these forty years in the wilderness, to humble you, and to prove you, to know what was in your heart, whether you would keep His commandments or not. He humbled you and let you suffer hunger, and fed you with manna, which you did not know, nor did your fathers know, that He might make you know that man does not live by bread alone; but man lives by every word that proceeds out of the mouth of the LORD.
>
> —DEUTERONOMY 8:1–3

God is a teacher, and His Law was to be a guidebook for His people. Is it any wonder, then, that when He came to earth, He came as a rabbi? Jesus came to teach us about God's kingdom. Because He was the ultimate fulfillment of the Law, He came to raise the standard for those in His kingdom—and so while He was on earth, He taught about this heavenly standard. This is why so often He began teachings on the kingdom with, "You have heard it said…" Jesus would then quote directly from the Law, whether it dealt with divorce proceedings, business dealings, or simply issues of forgiveness and love. Yet Jesus would always follow this by presenting a higher standard: "You have heard it said…but I say to you…" The "new" Law of His kingdom was not in contrast to God's original Law; it was the completion of it. Jesus was the embodiment of God's grace, love, mercy, and countless other attributes. Therefore, those who followed Him—new "citizens" of His kingdom—were covered by His grace and eventually empowered by His Spirit to obey this new Law of heaven, which Paul called "the law of the Spirit of life" (Rom. 8:2).

Before we move on, I want to highlight another major facet of the Law. In the Old Testament, God actually used the Law as a tool to communicate to His people. Do you remember how Israel begged Moses at the foot of Mount Sinai to have a mediator instead of dealing directly with the Lord? Exodus 19–20, which we have looked at several times, recounts how the people were so terrified of God's presence, holiness, and awesome power that they cried out to their leader, "You speak to us, and we will listen, but do not let God speak to us, lest we die" (20:19). God still wanted to communicate with His people, so He used the Law (in addition to Moses, who was already serving as the Lord's mouthpiece to Israel). Later, He also spoke through judges, priests, and kings, and eventually He spoke through the national prophets He appointed. Yet throughout all these phases, and even through the four hundred years of silence between Micah and John the Baptist, God still used the Law as His way of communicating, teaching, and guiding.

When Jesus came as the completion of the Law, God's desire was fulfilled: He was speaking directly to His people! God in the flesh could now communicate directly to Israel. This is one of the reasons why Jesus taught so much; God the Son was serving as the ultimate teacher once more, instructing His people on His ways, and guiding them further into His truth.

The Lord also knew that once He left in the flesh, His people would still need a teacher and guide. They would need to be reminded of truth, of the ways of His kingdom, and of the countless other things He had taught them (what future generations would read in the Scriptures). They would need a helper to know how to apply what they had learned in their everyday lives. So God graciously sent the Holy Spirit. Now the new law—a law of the Spirit, covered with grace—could dwell within them through the fulfillment of Jesus.

Jesus comforted His followers when He said, "The Counselor, the Holy Spirit, whom the Father will send in My name, will teach you everything and remind you of all that I told you" (John 14:26). And later Jesus explained even more: "When the Spirit of truth comes, He will guide you into all truth. For He will not speak on His own authority. But He will speak whatever He hears, and He will tell you things that are to come" (16:13). How incredible it is to realize that we now have the greatest teacher ever—the very Spirit of God—living inside of us, available every moment to instruct and guide us in His ways!

PURPOSE 4: TO CALL US TO GRACE

If you have not already noticed, it is difficult to accurately explain God's Law without also mentioning God's grace. As we saw in the previous chapter, the Law and grace really do go hand in hand. And this, in fact, is one of the Law's primary functions and purposes. God intended all along that the Law would draw people to Him. Remember, His desire has always been for relationship with His people. In His sovereign wisdom, God knew that it would take the Law for His people to experience Him more, even when they disobeyed. How is that possible? How could people experience God more through trying to obey commandments they could not keep (at least not all of them)? The Law itself calls people to grace!

The Law causes us to recognize that we cannot live up to God's holy call upon our lives in our own strength. Through the Law we recognize our own weakness and are confronted with our desperate need for grace and mercy. The Pharisees and religious leaders of Jesus' time were living proof that as soon as we think we are experts at following God's Law, pride will creep in and defile our hearts. The Law humbles us and forces us to recognize our inability to fulfill it on our own.

In the same way, the Law also brings to light those things we often would prefer to hide. Through the Law comes the knowledge of sin. Paul's way of describing it is that "through the law we become conscious of our sin" (Rom. 3:20, NIV). Indeed, it takes the Law for us to be aware of how we have wronged God. Paul continues to explain this masterfully in his letter to the Romans:

> I would not have known what sin was had it not been for the law. For I would not have known what coveting really was if the law had not said, "You shall not covet."...So then, the law is holy, and the commandment is holy, righteous and good....We know that the law is spiritual; but I am unspiritual, sold as a slave to sin.
>
> —ROMANS 7:7, 12, 14, NIV

The problem, then, isn't the Law. Stated differently, the Law is not what makes us fail to live up to its standards. Instead, it is the sinful nature in us that makes each of us "a slave to the law of sin" (Rom. 7:25, NIV). That is what causes us to do the very things we do not want to do, the very things we despise.

> So I find this law at work: Although I want to do good, evil is right there with me. For in my inner being I delight in God's law; but I see another law at work in me, waging war against the law of my mind and making me a prisoner of the law of sin at work within me. What a wretched man I am! Who will rescue me from this body that is subject to death? Thanks be to God, who delivers me through Jesus Christ our Lord!
>
> —ROMANS 7:21–25, NIV

The only One who can rescue us from our sinful nature is Yeshua, and the fact that He longs to rescue us is pure grace. We do not deserve to be saved; we deserve punishment—death, in fact—since we are violators of God's holy Law. We all stand guilty before the Lord. And yet rather than receiving the rightful punishment of death, we have received eternal life through Jesus Christ. *That* is grace in the form of a person!

When we appeal to God for salvation, we open the gates of our lives to allow Jesus to come in and flood us with grace. Without Him, without His grace, we would not have a chance. Yet because God's grace was expressed in the perfect form of His Son dying on the cross for us, we now can live through Him. In this beautiful way not only does the Law call us to grace, but it calls us to the very person who *is* grace: Yeshua HaMashiach.

Purpose 5: To Make Spiritual and Practical Application

The last purpose of the Law that I want to draw your attention to involves its spiritual and prophetic nature. We must remember that although we are not under the Law, the Law is still holy and spiritual. As we just looked at, Paul said the Law "is holy and the commandment is holy and just and good" (Rom. 7:12). In verse 14, he calls the Law "spiritual." And as such it has application for our lives.

For example, consider Deuteronomy 22:8: "When you build a new house, you must make a guard rail for your roof so that you bring no blood guilt on your house, should anyone fall from there." In the days when the Torah was first given, people lived in homes with flat roofs. This was where they entertained visitors and spent time fellowshipping together as a family and with others. Children even played up there. Because God is so personal and cares deeply about His people, He even gave them a law so that no one would get hurt as they entertained and played on their roofs.

God wanted to be intimately involved in every detail of His people's lives, even to the extent of giving them instructions to safeguard their property. This is also why God said to Israel after giving them the Law, "And what nation is there so great that has statutes and judgments so righteous as all this law, which I am setting before you today?" (Deut. 4:8).

Now the reality is that people today in most parts of the world no longer build guard rails around their roofs. (And if you live in a subdivision, it's likely your HOA wouldn't even let you!) But is there a spiritual application to this Law that still applies to us today? I think so.

Simply put, God wants us to safeguard whatever property we hold authority over—both physically and spiritually. If we live in a climate where we get lots of snow and ice in the winter, we can practically apply this verse to mean we should put salt down on the steps of our property so no one will slip on the ice and hurt himself. In a spiritual sense, we are to take the same kind of caution as we look out for the well-being of others who come into our lives.

Another example of the Law's spiritual and practical application for our lives today is found in Deuteronomy 22:11. When God originally gave this law, He told His people, "You must not wear clothing made of a material of wool and linen together." Many commentators believe that the reason God gave Israel this law was because the heathen nations that surrounded them dressed in garments that contained both wool and linen. But God did not want His people to dress like the people around them; He wanted a people separated unto Him.

The application for us today, then, would be that the Lord does not want His people dressing like the world. We are to dress modestly in a way that reflects God's beauty and holiness and honors Him, as opposed to dressing provocatively to draw attention to ourselves and to elicit sexual impulses from others.

A BLESSING OR A CURSE?

It is far too easy for believers on this side of the cross to negate the Law that God gave Israel and nullify its purpose with so-called New

Testament theology. In our era of hyper-grace teaching and forgiveness without repentance, the Law has become a bad word in many church circles. But I hope that after reading this chapter, you can see the good the Law has done and still does. Jesus was careful to explain that He did not come to abolish the Law but to fulfill it. In the same way, we must realize that He did not come to cancel the Law but to cancel the *penalty* for breaking the Law. Colossians 2:14 says Jesus took that penalty and nailed it to the cross. The difference in wording between "cancel the Law" and "cancel the penalty of the Law" may be subtle, but the difference in meaning is huge. One completely negates what God established to bring His people closer to Him and what Paul called "holy and just and good" (Rom. 7:12); the other acknowledges the Law's inherent goodness while also recognizing its potentially damning outcome.

Such subtleties are easy to miss in a day when the Law is so often preached as irrelevant. Indeed, I believe the same type of clarification is needed when people believe that the Law is inherently a curse rather than a blessing. Today I hear many Bible teachers and preachers refer to the "curse of the law," quoting a phrase Paul used in Galatians 3. They describe all things related to the Law of Moses as cursed, and they essentially imply that God's original setup became a curse for Israel. This is a dangerous misunderstanding, and allow me to explain why I believe so by first quoting the entire passage:

> For all who rely on the works of the law are under the curse. For it is written, "Cursed is everyone who does not continue in all things which are written in the Book of the Law, to do them." Now it is evident that no man is justified by the law in the sight of God, for "The just shall live by faith." But the law is not of faith, for "The man who does them shall live by them." Christ has redeemed us from the curse of the law by being made a curse for us—as it is written, "Cursed is everyone who hangs on a tree"—so that the blessing of Abraham

might come on the Gentiles through Jesus Christ, that we
might receive the promise of the Spirit through faith.

—GALATIANS 3:10–14

This passage may sound confusing upon first reading, in part because of the various uses of the word *law*. If you have studied many
of Paul's letters, you will recognize this as a common dilemma in the
translation of his writings. Paul wrote in Greek, a language in which
there was no word for *legalism*. Because of this, he often relied on
his context to clarify whether his use of the word *law* was positive
or negative, or he would use phrases such as "the works of the law,"
which always had a negative connotation. In this passage, context is
the key to understanding whether he meant the curse derived from
the Mosaic Law or from a spirit of legalism.

In verse 10, Paul mentioned those who "rely on the works of the
law" to save them. These were people striving under the Mosaic Law
and believing their works would earn them favor with God. This is
legalism in action. Anyone striving to earn salvation through legalism was missing the Law's ultimate purpose of grace and therefore
was "under the curse," as Paul described it in verse 10. This, then, is
the context for verse 13, where Paul wrote of Jesus saving us from
"the curse of the law." The apostle had not suddenly shifted gears; this
was the same curse of legalism.

The reason I am spending time to explain this passage is because
there is a big difference between legalism and the Mosaic Law. Legalism, which is what Paul often meant in using the word *law* (with
a little *l*), is the result of sinners trying to use the Law itself to make
them more holy. (See Galatians 2:18.) For example, Jesus said the
Pharisees loved to make a big show when they prayed (Matt. 6:5).
They were obeying the Law yet using it to validate what they thought
would earn them points with God and others.

God intended the Law—with a capital *L*—to be a blessing, yet
the legalists turned it into a curse. In their sinfulness, they were cor-
rupting the Law's intent. Rather than receiving God's grace through
the Law of Moses and drawing closer to the Lord, they attempted

to save themselves through their own efforts of following the Law—
and in so doing, rejected God's grace.

We must be careful to avoid the same mistake. As Paul expressed
in Romans 7, our sinful nature easily distorts the Law that God intended to be good, and we can end up falling into the trap of spiritual pride or a works-based salvation. Yet the good news—no, the
wonderful news—is that the Law is no longer the goal. As wonderful
as it was, Jesus came to interpret the Law for us, and in teaching us
the higher ways of His kingdom, He made it clear what the goal is
now: *He* is the goal of the Law!

"I am the way and the truth and the life," Jesus said. "No one comes
to the Father except through me" (John 14:6, NIV). Though the Law
is good, it is no longer our means of getting closer to God; Jesus is.
And praise God, as the complete fulfillment of the Law, Jesus has already made the way through Him and to Him.

CHAPTER 11

GOD'S PLAN OF SALVATION

I HAD AN UNUSUAL fear of dying as a young boy. It was not something that gripped me daily or that I thought about all the time, but in retrospect my fears surrounding death went beyond the norm for someone my age. For example, during Safety Awareness Week at my elementary school, each student was supposed to create a poster that emphasized some theme concerning safety. Most of my classmates focused on things such as looking both ways before crossing a street, not playing with matches, or wearing a life preserver while swimming. But not me. I drew a medicine cabinet open with a pill bottle marked "POISON" and complete with an ominous skull and crossbones. The truth was that I was afraid that somehow I would get poisoned. My fear was so real that I worried about using our mercury thermometer for fear that I would accidentally drop it and the mercury would bounce off the floor, somehow get into my mouth, and instantly kill me. It was an absurd thought, yet in my head it was a serious matter—and as real as death itself.

As time went on, a new fear began to invade my life. It had to do with feeling lost and purposeless. I was only twenty years old, but I felt as if I was experiencing an identity crisis; I was desperately looking for meaning in my life. Until then I had built my adolescent life around wrestling. It had been my source of success and identity, and I had not considered what life might be like when I could no longer wrestle. Though I was offered a small scholarship to the University of Tampa, somewhere along the way reality hit me harder than an opponent throwing me face-first to the mat. I realized the world was bigger than my weight class. Wrestling could only take me so far in life; I needed something else to give me purpose.

With my wrestling dreams shattered, I thought about becoming a doctor. Many of my Jewish friends had this as their professional goal, so I thought maybe that would bring me the same type of success and fulfillment I had experienced in athletics. Upon deeper consideration I realized that I did not have the aptitude to become a doctor, so I thought becoming a lawyer was doable. Still something deeper gnawed at me. I was looking for a more permanent solution than just the right career choice.

That is when I discovered a copy of *Autobiography of a Yogi*, written by Paramahansa Yogananda. I will never forget reading the pages of that book and feeling as if I was being lifted far above the everyday concerns of life. The famous Indian guru wrote about having a personal relationship with a deity, and the pictures of him allegedly levitating fascinated me. He talked about inner peace found through meditation and a self-realization that could make me more aware of my "oneness" with God. Whatever I thought he had, I knew I wanted more than I wanted to make money or have a successful career.

I was well on my way to seeking inner peace through yoga and meditation when Jesus showed up. As I relayed earlier in this book, my radical encounter with Him came in 1978 when I was suddenly awakened from my sleep one night and saw Yeshua in a vision. He was hanging on the cross, and though He did not say anything to me, I will never be able to shake the deep imprint His presence left on my soul and spirit. I instantly knew that Jesus was the answer I had been searching for all along.

Over the next few days I found a copy of the New Testament and began devouring every page of it. I could not get enough, and an insatiable fire burned in me to know and experience Jesus more. I read in the B'rit Hadashah that if I believed in my heart and confessed with my mouth that Jesus is Lord, then I would be saved (Rom. 10:9). That sounded incredible to me, but I still had one question: What exactly was Jesus saving me from?

It was a legitimate question for me then and is the same question many Jewish believers face—for good reason. For all the common roots shared between Judaism and Christianity, one area where the two religions today stand vastly separated is the idea of salvation.

Christians base their faith on the premise that humanity is fallen, sinful, and separated from God. Jesus came to save us from eternal separation and, through His death and resurrection, made a way for each of us to be reconciled with God.

Judaism starts with a very different premise, however. Practicing Jews believe that personal salvation is irrelevant because we are not born into sin. They see salvation as merely a collective, national matter. Whenever the Tanakh speaks of the Lord's salvation, it is for the nation of Israel as a whole, not for the individual person.* Each person is believed to have a free will to do right and wrong, and when we sin, we are responsible for making things right with God through our own works.

As I read the New Testament more and more, I came to believe this was not true. I found that, just as Peter told the Sanhedrin in Acts, "There is no salvation in any other [than Jesus], for there is no other name under heaven given among men by which we must be saved" (4:12). I also found out this was not just a New Testament, "Christian" idea, but that the Tanakh revealed the same need for us to be saved through the blood of a perfect sacrifice—namely Yeshua HaMashiach.

Since Rabbinic Judaism's earliest days, the concept of personal salvation has been a stumbling block for many. Jews generally believe that you make amends for sin through three elements: repentance (*teshuvah*), good deeds (*mitzvot*), and a life devoted to God (*tefilah*). These are essentially what the Law is all about. How closely you follow the Law, then, serves as the major factor for how much you can avoid sinning, and therefore how close you are to God. Because Orthodox Jews strive to follow the Law as strictly as possible, they believe themselves to be the only stream of Jews following the "true" way, much like the Pharisees of Jesus' day.

Although most evangelical Christians do not adhere to a belief that we can work our way closer to God, I am always surprised by

---

* It is interesting how Judaism asserts this despite there being dozens of scriptures in the Tanakh where a writer personally refers to the Lord as "*my* salvation."

how many still believe Israel in the Old Testament earned its salvation this way. In fact, many people still teach today that God's chosen people in the Tanakh were saved through the Law—meaning through the God-established system of circumcision, sacrifice, and obedience to God's commands. In essence, these people believe that salvation in the Old Testament came through the Law, while salvation in the New Testament comes through faith.

As controversial as the topic may be, this is faulty teaching. God's plan for salvation has *always* been established by grace through faith alone. Again, He is the same God in the Old Testament as in the New Testament, and His plans for redeeming His people have not changed. Since the earliest times, God has always brought salvation through faith. The Israelites of old were saved by grace, through faith, and through a blood sacrifice, just as we are today as "New Testament believers." In this chapter we will look at many scriptures to prove this while also examining what God's plan of salvation actually entails. As we do this, I hope you can see more of how Jesus fulfills Judaism in every way as Israel's ultimate salvation.

SALVATION BY ELECTION

God made the first move.

When time did not exist, God began it. When the earth was formless, He put shape and order to it. And when God desired fellowship, He created humans in His own image. He took the initiative in creating us so that we might know Him and enjoy Him.

The principle of God's initiative is fundamental for us as we move through this chapter and address the issue of salvation. Simply put, salvation does not start—nor has it ever started, nor will it ever start—with us. When it comes to salvation, God takes the initiative, just as He took the initiative to start a relationship with us by forming us from dust.

When Adam and Eve sinned and brought separation between themselves and God, who was the one who pursued the other? God. In Genesis 3:9 the Lord called out to Adam while the man and his wife were attempting to hide from their Creator. Who was the one who made a way for restoration? God. Who was the one who, in His grace, covered Adam's and Eve's nakedness and shamefulness (Gen. 3:21)? God. The Lord started the first relationship with mankind, and He always took the initiative to keep that relationship intact.

Beginning with Adam, the Hebrew Bible is one continuous story of God reaching out to mankind. In Genesis 12 God called Abraham from a family of pagans and polytheists. We have no indication whatsoever that Abraham did anything special to merit God's attention. There is no mention of him being so righteous that it got God's attention from heaven. Given his family background, it is very likely Abraham was just another idol-worshipping heathen. Yet God chose him not because of his goodness or his works but because of the Lord's sovereign grace. Eventually God, through this ordinary man, would create a remnant for Himself among all the peoples of the earth, a portion of the global population that would remain devoted to Him. God made the first move and appeared to Abraham, establishing a covenant that continues to this day.

In the same way, God later chose Israel as His people not because of any goodness that they inherently possessed or because of their potential or anything else. In fact, Scripture tells us they were the least likely to be considered great, the "least of all peoples" (Deut. 7:7, TLV). Exodus 32:9 even describes them as a "stiff-necked" people. So obviously they did nothing to merit God's selection. Instead, the Lord chose them purely because He loved them. Deuteronomy spells this out in a beautiful way:

> For you are a holy people to the LORD your God. The LORD your God has chosen you to be His special people, treasured above all peoples who are on the face of the earth. The LORD did not set His love on you nor choose you because you were more in number than any of the peoples, for you were the fewest of all the peoples. But it is because the LORD

loved you and because He kept the oath which He swore to
your fathers.

—DEUTERONOMY 7:6–8

Just as it was with Abraham and Israel, none of us can earn God's
choice. God sovereignly chooses to give us faith because of *His* love,
not because of our deeds. This is grace in action. The Lord's sovereignty, combined with His divine choice—what is often called His
"election"—is the essence of what grace is. And salvation has always
been the result of God's sovereign grace.

Romans 9 highlights this exact point when recounting some of
the fathers of the faith, starting with Abraham's son, Isaac, and continuing through Jacob (who was renamed Israel, from which the nation of people also received their name).

> Rebekah also had conceived by one man, our father Isaac.
> For before the children had been born, having done neither
> evil nor good, *so that the purpose of God according to elec-*
> *tion might stand, not of works, but through Him who calls*, it
> was said to her, "The elder shall serve the younger."…What
> shall we say then? Is there unrighteousness with God? God
> forbid! For He says to Moses, "I will have mercy on whom
> I have mercy, and I will have compassion on whom I have
> compassion." So then it is not of him who wills, nor of him
> who runs, but of God who shows mercy.
>
> —ROMANS 9:10–12, 14–16, EMPHASIS ADDED

God shows mercy. *He* initiates our salvation. *He* is the "author
and finisher of our faith" (Heb. 12:2). We cannot forget that God
"desires all men to be saved and to come to the knowledge of the
truth" (1 Tim. 2:4). His heart's longing is for true relationship with
all people.

By mentioning this, however, I realize I have tapped into what can
be a tremendously confusing and difficult concept. It seems contra-
dictory that God has sovereign choice—meaning He chooses the
"elect" who are saved—and yet He still wants all to be saved. If He

wants all, then why does He choose only some? This is obviously not a book about this seemingly paradoxical nature of God, but I want to say from personal study and experience these two concepts can go hand in hand in God's character. God's sovereign election and His love for all are compatible. He is not a schizophrenic God, nor is He confused (1 Cor. 14:33).

Despite God reaching out to people and offering salvation in both biblical times and today, not everyone accepts His invitation. Obviously this is not breaking news to anyone; man has always been in opposition to God, and there have always been some who chose to reject Him. But notice how even in the face of such widespread rejection God still has always kept a remnant of faith in place. This once again highlights His extreme grace. Through all of Israel's cycles of disobedience, when God's "stiff-necked" people continued to rebel against Him after He had forgiven them time and time again, still God "preserved" a remnant for Himself (1 Kings 19:18).

In the same way, those brought into relationship with God today are the remnant, and we are in relationship because He chose us. "You did not choose Me, but I chose you," Jesus said in John 15:16. This was true for those before Christ—those in the Old Testament— and it is true today. We are saved by grace, which is a pure expression of the Lord's sovereignty and His choice.

SALVATION THROUGH FAITH

God's grace saves us, but we must also understand the role of faith in this salvation. Hebrews 11:6 tells us that "without faith it is impossible to please God." And yet the amazing truth is that faith does not come from us but from God Himself. God requires faith for salvation, and yet not only does He initiate this faith, but He also provides it! We cannot muster up faith, but we receive faith as a gift from God (Eph. 2:8).

Think again about God's original call to Abraham. What the Lord proposed to him sounded too good to be true: "I will make of you a great nation; I will bless you and make your name great, so that you will be a blessing. I will bless them who bless you and curse him who curses you, and in you all families of the earth will be blessed" (Gen. 12:2–3). Who wouldn't want this kind of a promise?

But have you ever thought about what God was actually asking of Abraham? The blessing was huge, but so was the cost. We find God's requirement in the previous verse: "Go from your country, your family, and your father's house to the land that I will show you" (Gen. 12:1). In short, God told Abraham to leave behind everything he had and everyone he knew and head to an undisclosed location. I wonder how long it took Abraham to decide to follow the Lord, whether he had to chew on it for a while or if he started packing right away. I would imagine he endured plenty of interrogations from family members while loading up his things. Most likely they disapproved and thought he was crazy for heading out to follow some invisible God.

"Abe, where in the world are you headed?"

"Um...I'm not quite sure."

"So who told you to go?"

"I don't really know."

"Then *why* are you going?"

"Well, um...it's hard to explain."

What would that kind of a move require? Faith! In fact, I would argue Abraham's response required some supernatural faith that came from somewhere—or someone—else. Though the Bible merely records in this instance that "Abram departed, as the LORD had spoken to him," later it mentions how faith was involved (Gen. 12:4). In Genesis 15:6, after God again visits Abraham and elaborates on His covenant promises, the Bible simply says, "Abram believed the LORD." Where do you think Abraham got this faith? From God!

When the Lord appeared to Abraham, He instilled faith in him— faith to step out into the unknown and trust an unseen God. Beloved, when we encounter the Lord, we cannot help but gain faith. Meeting a supernatural God results in supernatural faith. And when the power of God comes upon your life, faith springs forth. The King James Version of Psalm 110:3 says, "Thy people shall be willing in the day of thy power." The power of the Holy Spirit in our lives produces faith, just as it did in the lives of Abraham and David.

Ephesians 2:8 makes it clear that we do not naturally possess the kind of supernatural faith that saves, nor can we conjure it up: "For by grace you have been saved through faith, and *this is not of yourselves*" (emphasis added). So where does this faith come from? This verse and the next go on to explain: "It is the gift of God, not of works, so that no one should boast" (vv. 8–9).

God gave Abraham the gift of faith to believe Him, take Him at His word, and follow Him even when Abraham could not see the way and did not know where he was going. That faith was imparted to Abraham when God appeared to him.

What I want to highlight, however, is that faith has *always* been required for salvation, even in the Hebrew Bible. I already quoted from Genesis 15:6, which begins by simply stating that "Abram believed the LORD." Yet the verse continues with a fascinating statement, especially given that it is found in the Torah: "Abram believed the Lord, and He credited it to him as righteousness." What a remarkable concept! God made an exchange in Abraham's spiritual account: because of his faith, the Lord deposited some heavenly currency called righteousness in his name. Does this mean we earn righteousness? Not at all, because the Bible also says, "Not by works of righteousness which we have done, but according to His mercy He saved us" (Titus 3:5).

What this verse in Genesis shows us, then, is God's astonishing and unusual way of accounting. He took Abraham's faith—which the Lord had given to him in the first place—and because Abraham used that gift, He then turned it into "right standing with Him" (which is a simple way to define righteousness). In other words, Abraham's faith brought him closer to God!

It reminds me of playing make-believe "shopping" with children. If you have ever raised or babysat a little boy or girl, then you can almost certainly remember the fun a child can have playing with a simple set of plastic food items, a toddler-sized shopping cart, and a register (complete with play money). Children typically love it when you "shop" for food items at their store, "buy" those items from them, and then "eat" them in front of them—which typically involves making funny, exaggerated sounds to show them how amazing their food tastes.

To buy any of their items, however, you need money. So each time you enter a child's store, she will give you some of the fake money from her toddler-sized cash register. When you are done shopping, you then give her the money as if it were yours, and then the sequence repeats itself the next time you go "shopping" in her store.

Our exchange of faith with God is much the same. God supplies the faith for us to believe Him, which ultimately leads to salvation. And yet when we hand Him back what He gave us in the first place, He then delights in allowing us to enjoy the fruit as if we had supplied it in the first place. Amazing!

Abraham was not the only one whose faith was credited to him, nor was he the only one we find in the Hebrew Bible who was saved by faith. This concept is illustrated repeatedly in God's relationship with the nation of Israel. God saved Israel out of Egypt. We know this salvation did not come because they followed the Law, because the Law had not yet been given. Instead, Israel was saved through God's sovereign grace and through faith. After the Lord miraculously parted the Red Sea and Israel walked through to its salvation, Exodus 14:31 says, "When Israel saw the great power which the LORD used upon the Egyptians, the people feared the LORD, *and they believed in the Lord* and in His servant Moses" (emphasis added).

Again, why did God save them? Because He loved them. And because He loved them, He chose them and imparted faith to them.

Soon after Israel's salvation from Egypt, God gave them the Law because they were His chosen people. But it is essential for us to see that the Jewish people were first called to relationship with God; then later they were called to live an obedient lifestyle through the Law. The fruits of righteousness that came from obeying God's Law were secondary to the fruits of righteousness first gained from simply being in relationship with God. And that relationship began through the gift of faith, given by God.

Likewise, God does not save us today because we are holy and have followed His laws. Instead, He calls us to holiness—to the fruits of obeying His ways—because we are already His. Out of our relationship with Him comes obedience. But it is our relationship with Him—a relationship by grace through faith—that is the core of our salvation.

SALVATION THROUGH THE BLOOD COVERING

We are saved by grace through faith alone. This is the same way Abraham was saved, the same way Israel was saved, and the same way for all others throughout the Hebrew Bible. The grace of God comes to us, God reveals Himself to us, He stirs something in our hearts, and He puts faith in us. That is what it means when we say that *by grace* we are saved *through faith.* But if I were to stop there, our explanation of God's plan for salvation would be incomplete because even though we are saved by grace through faith alone, there is still more to the story; this is where we begin to see how Jesus completes the plan of salvation.

When God created humans, He wanted to walk with us just as He and Adam walked together in the Garden of Eden. He desires that kind of fellowship with us. But Adam and Eve created a problem when they disobeyed the Lord, one that has lingered ever since they left Eden: to walk in union with God, our sin must first be dealt with. Throughout human history the problem of sin and our sinful nature has been a dividing factor between the Lord and us. It is not just that our sinfulness is incompatible with God's holy nature; it is also that our sinful nature cannot handle His holiness.

The payment for sin was death. That is its natural cost. But to rectify this problem for His people, God set up a system of sacrifice. For an individual to avoid judgment, he had to "pay" for his own sin with the blood of an innocent one. This is why throughout the Old Testament we find that God's means of forgiving Israel's sins and protecting them from judgment was by the blood of an unblemished animal. The principle involved, called substitutional sacrificial atonement, was this: for a guilty person to be reunited with God and restored to a rightful relationship with Him, someone or something had to pay the price in exchange. But this payment could not be just anyone or anything; it had to be an *innocent* creature, who would then die in place of the guilty one in order for that person to be cleansed and made righteous again.

In Leviticus 17:11 the Lord told His people, "For the life of the flesh is in the blood, and I have given it to you on the altar to make atonement for your lives; for it is the blood that makes atonement for the soul." A person's life is bound up in his blood. So if his blood has been given through a sacrifice, that means his life has been taken. Simply put, the one whose blood has been given has died so that the one deserving of death could live.

This is the foundational premise of Passover, one of the most important times in Judaism. As part of the Jewish people's salvation from Egypt, the Lord warned them, "I will pass through the land of Egypt this night and will smite all the firstborn in the land of Egypt, both man and beast, and against all the gods of Egypt I will execute judgment" (Exod. 12:12). God commanded each household to take in an unblemished male lamb. If those living there wanted to avoid death and judgment when the Lord passed through Egypt, then they needed to kill the lamb, eat it, and put its blood over their doorpost. As the Lord came through, any house that was "covered in the blood" was deemed protected and was therefore not judged. All others suffered the consequences of death.

Later the Lord would once again establish a time when Israel could be "covered by the blood" and protected from the judgment it deserved for its sin. As great as Passover is for the Jewish people, Judaism's holiest and highest holiday of the year is Yom Kippur, which means the Day of Atonement. On that day the high priest would take an unblemished bull and two unblemished goats. First he would kill the bull, take its blood, and sprinkle it on the ark of the covenant, which is sometimes referred to as the mercy seat. When the Lord saw the bull's blood poured upon the ark, He would forgive the sins of the high priest and his family.

Then the priest would go outside and gather the two goats. He would cast lots to see which goat would be sacrificed to the Lord and which would be the *azazel*, or scapegoat. The sacrificed goat's blood would then be sprinkled over the ark of the covenant, only this time it was for the sins of all Israel for the entire year. Finally the priest would also lay his hands upon the scapegoat and confess all of Israel's sins. (I imagine this took some time!) The goat was then let go into the wilderness, where it was to "bear on it all their iniquities to a desolate land" (Lev. 16:22).

Interestingly enough all these ceremonial actions for cleansing required faith. The priest who entered the holy of holies, where the ark of the covenant was, had to be completely cleansed. This was where God's presence resided, and it was known that if a priest went in unclean, he would immediately die from the power of God's holiness. You better believe that whoever entered that room was going in faith! Likewise, the children of Israel had to have faith to believe they would be protected on Passover night as the Lord went through Egypt. They may have followed all the preparation instructions to a tee, just as the priest entering the holy of holies would have done, but ultimately they still had to have faith that God would save them, not their own works. In the same way, the Jewish people needed faith to believe that God would make amends for their sins by the actions on Yom Kippur. So even in this sacrificial system, which operated under the Law, the people still found salvation through faith.

This was the system God established—again, showing His mercy, grace, and love—so that His people could be cleansed of their sin, come close to Him, and enjoy the relationship He desired all along. And for hundreds of years this was the temple system of sacrifice that every Jew lived by. It was the same system Jesus was born into and what He engaged in throughout the year, as taught by His earthly parents. Can you understand more now why salvation for the practicing Jew is not seen as an individual thing but a collective identification? For the Jewish people, the exchanges at Yom Kippur and Passover were never about atoning for just one individual but always the entire nation of Israel.

But let me ask you an important question: Do you think the blood of the bull and goat were literally what saved Israel from being punished for their sins? Of course not! Those animals were not holy in themselves. They were not righteous, and therefore this was obviously not a perfect exchange of righteousness to take the place of sinfulness. The bulls, goats, and blood were mere *symbols* that God established as the acceptable payment for sin. God had instructed the Jewish people to offer those things; it was not as if they had suggested them in a brainstorming meeting with God about how to solve their national sin crisis. Once again, God made the first move by offering an acceptable solution.

What I want you to see, however, is that those symbols were mere placeholders for the real sacrifice: Jesus! The bulls, goats, and blood did not have any real value in and of themselves, yet God accepted them because He knew the actual payment—the real exchange— would come. It is similar to what we do with credit cards. When I buy something at a store, the store clerk will accept my credit card as payment because of what it represents. The card has no value in itself; it is simply a piece of plastic. But the clerk understands what my credit card symbolizes and means. I may not have any actual money to give the clerk at that point, but by my using a credit card, she knows the real payment is coming.

Hundreds of years after Passover, Jesus fulfilled the Passover exchange in an even greater way with His own death. Jesus went to the cross not just as a perfect person but as the very "Lamb of God, who takes away the sin of the world," as John the Baptist called Him, who was spotless in every way (John 1:29). God provided the necessary sacrifice: Himself! Jesus is forever "our Passover lamb" (1 Cor. 5:7, NIV). His death made it possible for each of us to "take Him in" by faith, just as the Jews would take in a lamb by faith before Passover. The Jews ate the Passover lamb, and in the same way we take in Jesus' body and blood, which is what the sacrament of Communion, or the Lord's Supper, is all about. And just as the Jews marked their doorposts with the blood of a spotless lamb, we can be covered by Jesus' blood, which was poured out freely on the cross for everyone. When we receive Jesus in faith, the spiritual doorposts of our lives are marked with His blood, which protects us from impending judgment.

Likewise, Jesus' blood fulfilled the Yom Kippur requirement of blood on the altar. (This is what Hebrews 8–10 is all about.) His sacrifice atoned for our sins and made a way to put us in union with God once more. And as the scapegoat, Jesus bore our sins away. As David prophesied in the Tanakh, "As far as the east is from the west, so far has He removed our transgressions from us" (Ps. 103:12).

One day, when all of creation stands before the great white throne spoken of in Revelation 20:11–15, God will judge the saved and unsaved, just as He judged all people—Jews and Gentiles—in Egypt on Passover. And like Israel at Passover, the only thing that will save us from God's eternal judgment at that point is if the blood of Jesus covers us, which will be proved by our names being in the Lamb's Book of Life, authenticating that He has saved and redeemed us.

God's way of salvation was not easy. It took an innocent to save a guilty. It took blood, the ultimate symbol of death, to bring about life. Ultimately it took His only Son sacrificed on our behalf. As unimaginably difficult as that was, He did it. And because of this amazing exchange, we can be restored once again to union with Him.

SALVATION THROUGH A MEDIATOR

At the foot of Mount Sinai, the children of Israel made a decision that shaped the rest of history. God longed to have a close relationship with His people, just as He had wanted since the Garden of Eden. He had brought salvation to the children of Israel by drawing them out of Egypt and miraculously providing for them in the desert. He had proved again and again that He would lead them, protect them, and bless them. And now, on the slopes of Sinai, He wanted to meet with them.

Sadly the Israelites were too afraid. God's presence was too terrifying for them. As soon as He showed up to speak with them—ushering in an awesome display of His power—the people had enough. Exodus records the scene:

> All the people witnessed the thunder and the lightning and the sound of the trumpet and the mountain smoking; and when the people saw it, they trembled and stood at a distance. They said to Moses, "You speak to us, and we will listen, but do not let God speak to us, lest we die."
>
> Moses said to the people, "Do not fear, for God has come to test you, so that the fear of Him may be before you so that you do not sin."
>
> [But] the people stood a distance away as Moses drew near to the thick darkness where God was.
>
> —Exodus 20:18–21

That last verse is haunting. Here was a chance to draw close to their God, who had already proved His love, grace, mercy, provision, and countless other things to the Jewish people. He desired to lead them in an intimate relationship, and yet they preferred to stay "a distance away." Just as importantly, they preferred to have Moses be their mediator rather than dealing directly with God themselves.

From that moment on things changed drastically for Israel. In fact, from that point Judaism became centered on the interaction between God and a mediator rather than the Lord dealing directly with His people. Even though Judaism believes in a God who has chosen the Jewish people as His own, still they are generally a people who often do not deal directly with their God. Just as the Jewish people during the time of the Torah left it up to Moses to deal with God on their behalf, today many Jews leave the responsibility of dealing with God to the rabbi.

God, in His mercy, accepted the Israelites' preference and established a system where He would meet only with selected representatives from the people.* These priests became the go-between figures

---

* We see this exchange repeated again when after the Jewish people were led into the Promised Land, God wanted to be their king and deal with the nation directly. But instead of dealing directly with God, Israel preferred to have an earthly king. (See 1 Samuel 8:1–22.)

for all of Israel, and their function was invaluable. When the Israelites offered sacrifices at the temple, they relied entirely upon the priests performing on their behalf. For example, Leviticus 23 records the layered interaction surrounding the wave offering:

> The LORD spoke to Moses, saying: Speak to the children of Israel, and say to them: When you have come into the land that I am giving to you and reap its harvest, then you shall bring a sheaf bundle of the first fruits of your harvest to the priest. And he shall wave the sheaf before the LORD so that you may be accepted.
>
> —LEVITICUS 23:9–11

How much greater (and easier) this would have been if God could have simply spoken and interacted directly with His people. But instead, He honored the people's request. Moses became the mediator and messenger for God, while the priests became the hands and feet for any spiritual activities.

As we saw in the last section, Yom Kippur highlighted Israel's dependence on a mediator more than any other time of the year. On that day the high priest, serving as the chief mediator, was the only one who could approach God's presence by going into the holy of holies. He sacrificed a bull and a goat and used their blood to atone for both his own sins and those of the people. But if the high priest made one wrong move in the sacrificial service, it affected the entire nation. Israel was at the mercy of the high priest doing it right. Talk about being utterly dependent on someone!

Putting this together then, we see that in the Old Testament, God set up a temporary system that allowed for priests to be the mediator between His people and Himself. But when Jesus came, He fulfilled this position more than any other human could have. As New Testament believers, we now have a High Priest (Jesus) who offered His own body and blood to atone for us. The writer of Hebrews brilliantly explains how Jesus, as the ultimate mediator for us, fulfilled not only the position of the priest offering blood sacrifices but also virtually everything else related to the temple system.

But Christ, when He came as a High Priest of the good
things to come, by a greater and more perfect tabernacle,
not made with hands, that is to say, not of this creation,
neither by the blood of goats and calves, but by His own
blood, He entered the Most Holy Place once for all, having obtained eternal redemption. For if the blood of bulls
and goats, and the ashes of a heifer, sprinkling the unclean,
sanctifies so that the flesh is purified, how much more shall
the blood of Christ, who through the eternal Spirit offered
Himself without blemish to God, cleanse your conscience
from dead works to serve the living God?

For this reason He is the Mediator of a new covenant,
since a death has occurred for the redemption of the sins
that were committed under the first covenant, so that
those who are called might receive the promise of eternal
inheritance.

—HEBREWS 9:11–15

As explained in the very next chapter, Jesus' sacrifice was for
not just one time but forever. Because of His ministry as our ultimate High Priest, we have been atoned through His sacrifice for
all eternity:

By this will we have been sanctified through the offering of
the body of Jesus Christ once for all.

But every priest stands daily ministering and repetitively
offering the same sacrifices, which can never take away sins.
But this Man, after He had offered one sacrifice for sins forever, sat down at the right hand of God. Since that time He
has been waiting for His enemies to be made His footstool.
For by one offering He has forever perfected those who are
sanctified.

—HEBREWS 10:10–14

Jesus fulfilled every priestly requirement for sacrifice that God established through the Law and the temple system of worship. It is
because of His actions that we can be reunited with God forever, just

as He desired. This was His original plan for salvation! As we end this chapter, I want to summarize some of what we have unveiled regarding Jesus' role as our mediator and what Hebrews reveals in further detail.*

As our mediator...

+ Jesus sympathizes with our weaknesses (Heb. 4:15).

+ Jesus helps us in our need (Heb. 4:16).

+ Jesus intercedes for us (Rom. 8:34; Heb. 7:25).

+ Jesus is the God-Man, able to save us (Heb. 2:5–18; Col. 2:9).

+ Jesus has paid a ransom for us (1 Tim. 2:5–6).

+ Jesus has taken away our sins by the covering of His blood (Heb. 9:11–14).

+ Jesus is seated in majesty (Heb. 1:3; 8:1).

Judaism has always had a mediator. And God, in His mercy, has provided the ultimate mediator. Jesus, the King of the Jews, is the final go-between bridging the gap between God and mankind. As 1 Timothy 2:5–6 says, "There is one God and one mediator between God and men, the Man Christ Jesus, who gave Himself as a ransom for all. This was the testimony given at the proper time." Jesus has fulfilled the role of a mediator, with all its functions and requirements.

The revelation that God gave to Moses was actually the gospel that Jesus and the apostles preached in its primitive form. Salvation for Israel began when God chose them. It continued when they saw God's glory revealed at Sinai, which produced in them faith. Yet their relationship with God required both a blood sacrifice and a mediator. And these were completely fulfilled in Yeshua HaMashiach. So you see, all the principles of salvation revealed to us in the B'rit

---

* I highly encourage you to do an in-depth study of the Book of Hebrews if you have not already. And if you have studied Hebrews, then at least reread chapters 7–10 before continuing in this book. These chapters are powerful reminders of all that Jesus has done for us.

Hadashah (New Testament) were first revealed to Moses and Israel in embryonic form. God's plan of salvation has never changed, and it continues today both for Jews and Gentiles. Not only does Yeshua HaMashiach complete Judaism, but He *is* salvation for all!

CHAPTER 12

THE NEW COVENANT

YOU DO NOT have to be a theologian to understand the theological principle called progressive revelation. It may sound fancy, but I promise you it's not. However, it is important. Progressive revelation is the idea that God reveals Himself increasingly over time rather than all at once. This means the will of God and His eternal purposes are understood more fully as time goes by.

For example, we have already looked at how God established a sacrificial system in the Old Testament to deal with the issue of sin. According to God's Law, every sin warranted a punishment of some type, and the only way for a person who had sinned to avoid that punishment was for an innocent animal to take his place in receiving the due penalty. When Jesus came and died for our sins, we received a greater revelation of this concept. We find similar examples of progressive revelation throughout the New Testament as the revelation of God becomes clearer as time unfolds and crystallizes in the person of Jesus.

Paul described the idea of progressive revelation in Romans when he told the believers there that he had preached the gospel "according to the revelation of the mystery, which was kept secret for long ages past, but now is revealed by the prophetic Scriptures according to the commandment of the everlasting God" (Rom. 16:25–27). What before had been "kept secret" was now being revealed to the Gentile believers of Rome.

Likewise, the writer of Hebrews says, "God, who at various times and in diverse ways spoke long ago to the fathers through the prophets, has in these last days spoken to us by His Son, whom He has appointed heir of all things, and through whom He made the world" (Heb. 1:1–2). Both these scriptures show how during the period in which the Old Testament was being written, revelations of God were like shafts of sunlight breaking into a dark room. Yet now the ceiling has been lifted off the room and through Yeshua the fullness of the sun is shining upon us. This is the New Testament era in which we live.

Scripture has always involved progressive revelation. That means we have the privilege of seeing new facets of God in the Hebrew Bible today that could not be seen by those who lived during the Old Testament days. For example, God's grace is being revealed today in a greater way than during Moses' time because we live after the fullness of grace itself, Jesus the Messiah, came to earth. This is progressive revelation, which always points to Jesus.

THE COVENANTS OF OLD

One of the primary places we see progressive revelation at work in the Bible is in the covenants made by God. Although Scripture records others, there are three foundational covenants revealed in God's Word. It is important that we look at each one to better understand which elements of these covenants apply to our lives today and to see how Jesus is the culminating point of each one.

The first foundational covenant came through Abraham and is found in Genesis 12. God approached Abraham amid his pagan culture and said, "I will make of you a great nation; I will bless you and make your name great, so that you will be a blessing. I will bless them who bless you and curse him who curses you, and in you all families of the earth will be blessed" (vv. 2–3). This was an unconditional covenant, completely initiated and upheld by the Lord; God required nothing of Abraham for this covenant to be in effect. He did, however, repeat and rephrase His covenant to Abraham a few times after that, including the promise that "through your seed all the nations of the earth shall be blessed" (Gen. 22:18, AMP).

Isn't it interesting that God specifically said He would bless all the nations of the earth through a single seed? That seed was His own Son, Jesus. Hundreds of years before Jesus came to earth, God already knew that Jesus, the single "seed," would fulfill His covenant to Abraham. Paul explains this in Galatians 3:16 when he says, "Now the promises were made to Abraham and his Seed. He does not say, 'and to seeds,' meaning many, but 'and to your Seed,' meaning one, who is Christ."

Progressive revelation allows us to see now what Abraham could only hold in faith during his lifetime: that Jesus would be the fulfillment of God's covenant to him. Before Yeshua was born, the Israelites were the only people with the true revelation of who God was. Yet God wanted all peoples to know Him. His plan was not to restrict the revelation of Himself to just one group but that through Israel salvation would come to every tribe, tongue, and nation of the world. So we see in the Abrahamic covenant the promise of the Messiah, through whom all the nations of the world would be blessed; this is why the Abrahamic covenant is considered *the* foundational covenant.

The next foundational covenant came through Moses but was a pact to all the Jewish people. Unlike God's unconditional covenant to Abraham, the Mosaic covenant was conditional and promised either blessings or curses, depending entirely on Israel's actions.

> See, I am setting before you today a blessing and a curse: the blessing if you obey the commandments of the LORD your God, which I am commanding you today, and the curse, if you will not obey the commandments of the LORD your God, but turn from the way which I am commanding you today, to go after other gods which you have not known.
> —DEUTERONOMY 11:26–28

Throughout the Book of Deuteronomy the Lord repeatedly reminded His people, Israel, of the same message: follow Me, obey My ways, and I will bless you. In fact, His heart to bless is overwhelming, as Deuteronomy 28:1–14 depicts. If the Jewish people followed His ways, the Lord promised to bless their children, crops, animals, work, food, weather, finances, and many other things. God promised the Israelites that they could be a people so abundantly blessed that other nations would envy them for His favor upon them. He wanted His people to shine like blazing stars amid the darkness of the sinful nations surrounding them. In short, if the children of Israel would fulfill their part of the Mosaic covenant, they would be a beacon of God's salvation upon the earth, drawing all nations to Himself through the Jewish people.

But there was another side to this covenant—after all, it was conditional. If the children of Israel disobeyed God and did not obey His Law, then they would face the exact opposite consequences. For everything God said they would be blessed in, they would instead be cursed in—from their families to their work to their finances and even their weather. Though God had much to say in Deuteronomy regarding all the wonderful blessings His people could receive, He spent even more time warning them of the terrible consequences that would happen if they went their own way.

We know how the story ended. The tragic reality is that the very covenant God desired to be a blessing for His people instead became a curse. The covenant became like a millstone around their necks because no one was able to live in the obedience necessary to receive the blessings God wanted to give. Yet we can see now—once again through progressive revelation—that this was actually one of the purposes of both the Mosaic covenant and the Law. Both the Law and the covenant that undergirded it were to be our tutors to prepare us to meet Jesus (Gal. 3:24). Through the Law, God wanted His people to depend on Him. Romans 3:20 says the Law brings about "the knowledge of sin," and so God wanted the Law to cause His people to realize their deep need for His mercy and grace. It was impossible for them to fulfill the Law in their own strength, and therefore they could not receive the blessings of the covenant by their own efforts.

Yet even within the Law itself, God made a way for grace to be enacted through the sacrificial system. The Israelites could humbly present themselves before God, offer the sacrifices He desired while depending on His mercy, and receive freely from Him. God wanted to teach them through the Mosaic covenant and the Law how to depend on Him and His grace.

Jesus addressed such a posture in His parable about the Pharisee and the tax collector praying in the temple. (See Luke 18:9–14.) The Pharisee thanked God that he was not like the low-life sinners he saw around them, and reminded the Lord of all the "holy" fasting and tithing he had done. "But the tax collector, standing at a distance, would not even lift his eyes to heaven, but struck his chest, saying, 'God, be merciful to me a sinner'" (v. 13). Guess which one Jesus said was "justified" and made right with God? The humble tax collector who recognized his need for God's mercy (v. 14).

Even in this parable Jesus was prophetically highlighting how He was the fulfillment of the Law. He came for those who had no chance to be justified (i.e., all of us), yet the requirement on our part was to humbly receive God's grace and mercy, offered through the person of Jesus. The Pharisee in Jesus' story was too proud not only to recognize his real need but also to receive a free gift. His spiritual pride blinded him to the truth.

How often do we obstruct God from blessing our lives because we believe we can do things on our own? How often do we approach Him boasting in our own efforts: "God, have You noticed all the great things I've done for You lately? Have You seen all the people who were so moved when I led worship? What did You think when I gave my testimony—wasn't it great, Lord? Or how about when I helped that poor lady or gave money to those missionaries?" I pray that is not your typical way of thinking, but I know the reality is that all of us are prone to pride at different degrees.

No matter how humble we are before God, we always need His mercy. God's covenant with Moses served to point Israel to Jesus by teaching them about their need for Him as the fulfillment of the covenant, just as it does for us today. Only by living in Christ are we capable of experiencing God's abundant blessings, and yet through Him we have access to "every spiritual blessing in the heavenly places" (Eph. 1:3).

GOD WITH US, GOD IN US

Not only does the third and final foundational covenant point to Jesus, but also it came directly through Him. During the last Passover meal Jesus shared with His twelve disciples, He made what probably seemed at the time to be a party-killer announcement. Only days before, the disciples had seen their rabbi enter Jerusalem to the praises of His followers, who gave Him the Jewish red-carpet treatment and shouted, "Blessed is the King who comes in the name of the Lord!" (Luke 19:38). Shortly after, the Lord had cleansed the temple of merchants in a powerful display that probably had them wondering if this was when Jesus would finally ascend the throne, liberate the Jewish people from Roman oppression, and restore the kingdom of Israel. Now it was Passover, a joyous celebration of Israel's liberation from Egypt. In short, the disciples were likely in a festive mood.

Yet here was Jesus at the Passover meal first predicting that one of His disciples would betray Him, which instantly changed the mood, and then speaking soberly about His suffering and death. "I have earnestly desired to eat this Passover with you before I suffer. For I tell you, I will never eat it again until it is fulfilled in the kingdom of God" (Luke 22:15–16).

"Um…OK then," the disciples probably thought. "Jesus really needs something to lift His spirits."

"Then [Jesus] took the bread, and when He had given thanks, He broke it and gave it to them, saying, 'This is My body which is given for you. Do this in remembrance of Me'" (Luke 22:19).

"What…is…He…talking…about?" I can picture the disciples looking around at one another, clearly perplexed as the mood went from somber to downright ominous.

"Then He took the cup, and after He gave thanks, He gave it to them, saying, 'Drink of it, all of you. For this is My blood of the new covenant, which is shed for many for the remission of sins'" (Matt. 26:27–28).

When Jesus mentioned His blood, I wonder if any of the disciples got scared and started eyeing the exit. "We're to do what? Drink Your blood?" It's not hard to imagine that the room was deathly still. No one dared to say a word.

Many people read this passage in Luke as if Jesus and His disciples were acting out a well-rehearsed movie scene, because unfortunately that is the sense some believers have today when observing the Lord's Supper or Communion. It can feel like a scripted ceremony. And yet we must remember that for the disciples, this was happening in real time. What was supposed to be a festive meal seemed to quickly go south, with Jesus' every move now both symbolic and prophetic. At this point the disciples were surely familiar enough with their rabbi to know when He was offering a teaching moment, yet this seemed weightier than normal.

Jesus' mention of drinking His blood would have grabbed the disciples' attention, but His mention of a new covenant would have completely captured it. As young Jewish men, they had been raised to know God's covenants with Israel, each of which carried great significance. Any mention of a "new covenant" by the one they believed was the Son of God would have had them waiting with bated breath. It is likely they were studied enough in the Tanakh to immediately recall a similar phrase the great prophet Jeremiah had used in a prophecy almost six hundred years earlier:

> Surely, the days are coming, says the LORD, when *I will make a new covenant* with the house of Israel and with the house of Judah. It will not be according to the covenant that I made with their fathers in the day that I took them by the hand to bring them out of the land of Egypt, because they broke My covenant, although I was a husband to them, says the LORD. But this shall be the covenant that I will make with the house of Israel after those days, says the LORD: *I will put My law within them and write it in their hearts*; and I will be their God, and they shall be My people. They shall teach no more every man his neighbor and every man his brother, saying, "Know the LORD," for they all shall know

Me, from the least of them to the greatest of them, says the
LORD, for I will forgive their iniquity, and I will remember
their sin no more.

—JEREMIAH 31:31–34, EMPHASIS ADDED

In the Mosaic covenant, God literally wrote His Law on stone tablets. He delivered the Law atop Mount Sinai, and the tablets became
a national treasure housed in God's tabernacle. Yet in Jeremiah, He
promised a new covenant, different from the one delivered through
Moses. He would not write the law on stone tablets for His people, but
this time He would "write it in their hearts," putting His law "within
them" (v. 33). God would work from the outside to the inside. His law
would be housed in a new tabernacle: the very hearts of His people!

How would God do this, given that His people so often had
turned their hearts from Him? Ezekiel, who also lived around 600
BC, prophesied about this very thing: "I will give you a new heart,
and I will put a new spirit in you. I will take out your stony, stubborn heart and give you a tender, responsive heart. And I will put
my Spirit in you so that you will follow my decrees and be careful to
obey my regulations" (Ezek. 36:26–27, NLT).

Not only would God write His law on the hearts of His people, but
He would replace their hearts, which had become as hardened as the
stone tablets, with hearts of flesh that could feel and be sensitive to *His*
heart. His law would be inside them, in the tabernacle of their hearts,
and instead of His Spirit hovering over the tabernacle as it was in Moses'
time, God would now put His very Spirit inside His people. They would
become His temple, containing both His Spirit and His law!

Do you remember what God's original desire was at Mount Sinai?
He wanted to be close to His people. He wanted intimacy, to walk
closely with them as their God. Though the Israelites rejected His
initial invitation to come near to Him and instead asked for Moses
to be their mediator, the Lord patiently waited generation after generation as His children wandered farther away from Him, becoming
more self-reliant and trying to follow the Law on their own. During
this time God used numerous prophets to convey His desire to be

close to His people, and He even gave them promises for the future. In the Book of Isaiah, He promised He would send a Messiah whose very name would be Emmanuel, meaning "God with us" (7:14). And through Jeremiah and Ezekiel (and others), God promised that He would not just live with them, but He would live *in* them. His new covenant would include His very Spirit living *inside* His people.

POWER IN THE BLOOD

Let's go back to Jesus' final meal and see how the prophecies we have just mentioned connect to His declaration of a new covenant. During that meal, Yeshua gave His disciples bread and told them, "Take and eat. This is My body"; and He gave them the wine and said, "Drink of it, all of you" (Matt. 26:26–27). These elements were symbolic of His followers "taking in" God Himself. God was not content to be on the outside; He wanted to be so fully received in the deepest parts of His people that it was as if they ingested Him like food.

But if we look deeper at Jesus' last supper, we find yet another element worth pointing out. In every Gospel account of this meal, Jesus specifically associates the new covenant with His blood. "This cup is the new covenant in My blood which is shed for you," He says in Luke 22:20. Why was the blood so significant for this new covenant?

The answer to that question is actually found in the Law that was part of the "old" covenant of Moses. Remember that the Lord said in Leviticus 17:11, "For the life of the flesh is in the blood, and I have given it to you on the altar to make atonement for your lives; for it is the blood that makes atonement for the soul." Through the Law, God declared a powerful principle, namely that life was in the blood. The blood of an animal represented its life. Therefore, when an animal was sacrificed to atone for a person's sins, its blood was what truly mattered. This is why the blood was placed on the horns and base of the altar at the tabernacle when Aaron the high priest made atonement for himself and the sins of Israel (Lev. 9:1–9). The blood "covers" God's people, making them righteous before God.

When Jesus' blood was shed on the cross, it meant that His life was given. His blood represented His very life and was the most powerful reminder of the Law's sacrificial system: The innocent had to die for the guilty so the guilty could go free. Under the Law, an innocent animal, which did not deserve to die, would be sacrificed in place of a guilty person, who did not deserve to live. At the cross, Yeshua, the One who did not deserve to die, died in our place, and through His blood we who did not deserve to live were made alive and righteous before God.

Jesus' blood was not just symbolically shed for His disciples at the last supper; it was literally poured out for all mankind on the cross, making a way for every person to enter into this amazing new covenant. Just as the unblemished animal on the altar made a way for Israel's sins to be forgiven, Jesus' death on the cross as the perfect Lamb of God made a way for us to be reunited with God despite our sin. We now have the opportunity to enter the holy of holies—and into a relationship with God. Hallelujah!

FROM OLD TO NEW

I realize this chapter has been packed with potentially new information or insight for you, so as we conclude, let's review the three foundational covenants in the Bible. First came the Abrahamic covenant, a primary covenant that was based entirely on faith. Scripture says Abraham "believed God, and it was credited to him as righteousness" (Rom. 4:3; Gal. 3:6; see Gen. 15:6). Biblical faith is demonstrated by action, and Abraham's faith was proved by his obedience to God. His faith propelled him to take action. Again, Abraham was not saved by the Law, for the Law had not yet been given, yet he was counted as righteous because he believed God.

It is important to remember, however, that Abraham's faith was a gift from God, as we explored in the previous chapter. God had both appeared and spoken to him, which created faith in Abraham. He was saved by grace through faith, just as we are. As Ephesians 2:8–9 says, "For by grace you have been saved through faith, and this is not of yourselves. It is the gift of God, not of works, so that no one should boast."

The second foundational covenant is the Mosaic covenant. This temporary administrative covenant held Israel together until the fulfillment of the Abrahamic covenant came, which was Jesus. The Abrahamic covenant was based on faith and was unconditional. When God promised Abraham that He would bless him and his descendants, it was a done deal, and when the Lord promised that through Abraham's seed all the nations would be blessed, there was no question as to it coming to pass. That was the covenant, and it did not depend on Abraham or anything else. There were no further conditions from Abraham's part that needed to be met.

In contrast, the Mosaic covenant was not based on faith, nor was it unconditional. It was predicated upon Israel keeping the Law. (See Galatians 3:12.) This covenant kept Israel unified as a nation so that the Messiah could be born through God's first-covenant people. (See Genesis 49:10.) The Mosaic covenant also prepared the whole world for Jesus by teaching us that no man can earn God's favor or become righteous by keeping the Law on his own. Once Messiah came, the Law had served its primary purpose. As the writer of Hebrews says, "In speaking of a new covenant [Jesus] has made the first one old. Now that which is decaying and growing old is ready to vanish away" (v. 13). The Law and the Mosaic covenant are no longer the focal point; Messiah Yeshua is!

When Yeshua lifted the cup after the last supper and told His disciples, "This cup is the new covenant in My blood which is shed for you," I am certain all heaven paid attention (Luke 22:20). More than two thousand years after God gave His foundational covenant to Abraham, the time of its fulfillment had finally come. God had held Abraham's descendants together through generation after generation with the Mosaic covenant. Israel and the world had been prepared to receive God's ultimate solution, Yeshua the Messiah. What the Abrahamic covenant promised had manifest, and what the Mosaic covenant could not do Jesus, God's Son, did. His blood would be the ultimate proof of a new way of life—eternal life. Now, through Him and in Him not only are all the promises of God fulfilled; they are an eternal "Yes" and "Amen" (2 Cor. 1:20).

CHAPTER 13

ANCIENT PROPHECIES

T HROUGHOUT THIS BOOK we have looked at many scriptures from the Hebrew Bible that were later fulfilled through Yeshua HaMashiach. Often the New Testament reflects or elaborates on these fulfillments, explaining how Christ was the completion of their original purpose and how "all the promises of God find their Yes in him" (2 Cor. 1:20, ESV). For example, when the Book of Hebrews speaks at length of Jesus being our High Priest, it refers to numerous passages from the Tanakh, showing how Yeshua is the fulfillment of the original sacrificial system God established through the Torah.

In this chapter I want to narrow our focus specifically to the Messianic prophecies that Yeshua fulfilled throughout the Tanakh. One of the primary goals of this book is to reveal how Jesus fulfills every element of biblical Judaism; therefore I would argue this might be the most important chapter for any Jewish person reading this book. Many Jews have grown up in a cultural setting where they are simply told Jesus is not the Messiah, yet they have never actually looked at His life, much less searched the Scriptures, to see if that is true. For those who actually have examined the Tanakh's Messianic prophecies, their arguments and objections for believing that Yeshua is God's Son almost always stem from a single core claim on their part: Jesus did not fulfill all the Messianic prophecies of the Tanakh; therefore He cannot be the Messiah.

If you were to dig a little deeper with these unbelieving Jews, you would discover most make this claim based on the arguments that Jesus did not establish global peace, did not build a third temple, did not gather all Jews back to Israel, and did not unite the world under the knowledge of God. Therefore He must not be the Messiah, they claim.

One of the fundamental Christian beliefs, however, is that Jesus is coming back again, and this belief links directly to these four Jewish objections, all of which have to do with the end times. Christians do not argue that these four prophecies must be fulfilled, but they believe Jesus will complete them (and other biblical prophecies) upon His return. For the Christian, the fact that these prophecies remain unfulfilled does not mean Jesus was not the Messiah, because the Bible actually speaks of the Messiah in two forms: first as a suffering servant, and second as a mighty king.

Christians believe Jesus came first as a suffering servant to atone for our sins but that He will return as a mighty king to remove evil and rule over a new earth. Although the specific qualifications for the Messiah differ within Judaism (and always have), the Tanakh itself speaks of these two elements of the Messiah—as the suffering servant (Son of Joseph) and as the mighty king (Son of David).

Because the latter deals with future events that neither Christianity nor Judaism can verify (since none of us have lived through the end times), I want to spend the bulk of this chapter examining the Hebrew Bible's core passage that depicts Jesus as the suffering servant, Isaiah 53. In addition, I will point to the New Testament fulfillment of each of the prophecies given in that passage.

Yet Isaiah 53 is certainly not the only place in the Tanakh filled with Messianic prophecies. The Torah (Moses' books), Nevi'im ("prophets"), and Ketuvim ("writings") all contain numerous references, allusions, and predictions about HaMashiach. As previously stated, some scholars list as many as four hundred-plus Messianic prophecies throughout the Hebrew Bible.[1] To give us some context before diving into Isaiah 53, let's look at some of the major prophecies from this massive list that Jesus fulfilled:

+ The Messiah would be God (Isa. 9:6–7; Matt. 1:22–23).

- The Messiah would be called God's Son (Ps. 2:1–12; 1 John 5:20).

- The Messiah would be born of a virgin (Isa. 7:14; Matt. 1:22–23).

- The Messiah would be born in Bethlehem (Mic. 5:2; Matt. 2:1–2, 5–6).

- The Messiah would be a descendant of Abraham, Isaac, and Jacob (Gen. 12:1–3; Matt. 1:1–2).

- The Messiah would be a descendant of David (Ezek. 34:23; 37:24; Rev. 22:16).

- The Messiah would be from the tribe of Judah (Gen. 49:10; Rev. 5:4–10).

- The Messiah would be called the Son of Man (Dan. 7:13–14; Matt. 24:30).

- The Messiah, Abraham's seed, would bless the world (Gen. 22:18; Acts 3:25).

- The Messiah would be a prophet like Moses (Deut. 18:15–19; Acts 3:22–24).

- The Messiah would be preceded by Elijah (Mal. 3:1; Matt. 3:1–3; 11:10–11, 14).

- The Messiah would enter Jerusalem on a donkey (Zech. 9:9; Matt. 21:6–11).

- The Messiah would be pierced and crucified (Ps. 22:16; Zech. 12:10; Mark 15:22–25).

- The Messiah would be crucified without any bones broken (Exod. 12:46; John 19:33–36).

- The Messiah would be resurrected (Ps. 16:8–10; Acts 13:34–35).

+ The Messiah would institute the new covenant (Jer. 31:31–34; Heb. 8:8–12).

This list of Messianic prophecies is by no means exhaustive, but because this book focuses on how the Old and New Testaments connect, I wanted to show you how intricately and incredibly Yeshua fulfills the Messianic prophecies of the Tanakh. When you see this, it becomes almost unbelievable that so many in the church throughout the ages have been blinded to the Hebrew roots of their Christian faith. Jesus was not born two thousand years ago in a vacuum, but He literally stepped out of the pages of the Hebrew Bible in living flesh. This is why He was crucified with the sign over His head that read "YESHUA HA-NATZRATI, THE KING OF THE JEWS" (John 19:19, TLV).

PROPHETIC DIVISION

Perhaps no passage of Scripture within the Hebrew Bible divides practicing Jews and Christians as much as Isaiah 53. Whereas Christians see this passage as blatantly describing Jesus as the Messiah, most practicing Jews today have been taught that Isaiah 53 is about the nation of Israel rather than one specific person, and therefore it is incorrect to apply any significance to parallels between the passage and Jesus' life.

It is true that Isaiah 53 comes in the context of prophecies about the Jewish people's return from Babylonian captivity. Isaiah 52 and 54 clearly deal with this historical situation and apply to Israel as a nation. However, even a surface reading of Isaiah 53 can prove it is logically impossible to interpret the entire chapter in a national context, and the more you dive into the text, the more you see this as the case.

In addition, it should be noted that Jewish rabbis did not begin interpreting Isaiah 53 in any way other than referring to the Messiah until more than a thousand years after Jesus lived. That means that for the seventeen hundred years after Isaiah wrote this passage, Judaism's leaders—including the Talmud's writers, as well as those who wrote most of Judaism's foundational documents and interpretations—*never once* interpreted Isaiah 53 in a nationalistic way but believed it was about the Messiah. This remained true even while Christianity grew, while Jewish religious leaders attempted to unify people around a "new Judaism," and while both the chasm and the animosity between Judaism and Christianity expanded. You would think that in an attempt to defend Judaism and debunk Christianity (as many Jews would have done throughout the first centuries of the rising Christian church), at least *one* rabbi or Jewish leader would slant the interpretation of Isaiah 53 away from the Messianic viewpoint. And yet history proves that was not the case.[2]*

I also find it fascinating that many synagogue calendar readings in recent generations have omitted Isaiah 53, particularly if it is indeed such a key national prophecy. Could the omission be because of the controversy surrounding it, or the fact that many Messianic Jews point to this Scripture passage as one of the factors that led them to believe in Yeshua as HaMashiach? Jewish scholar Claude Montefiore acknowledged the controversy, saying, "Because of the christological interpretation given to the chapter by Christians, [the passage] is omitted from the series of prophetical lessons for the Deuteronomy Sabbaths...the omission is deliberate and striking."[3]

Rabbinic Judaism rejects that Jesus is the Messiah, yet because Isaiah 53 so clearly portrays Yeshua as, in fact, the Anointed One, the rabbis fear that the Jewish community may indeed read the passage, recognize that it points to Jesus, and put their faith in Him.

THE SUFFERING SERVANT, THE SORROWFUL SAVIOR

Having addressed the common objections from many Jews about Isaiah 53, I hope you can see why it is so significant. Few passages—much less entire *chapters*—in the Tanakh contain so many Messianic prophecies that the B'rit Hadashah itself verifies. So let's now dive into the verses of Isaiah 53, or what is often considered the

---

* For a more in-depth study on this and other common objections from Jews, I highly recommend Michael L. Brown's five-volume series, *Answering Jewish Objections to Jesus.*

Hebrew Bible's greatest depiction of the Messiah. I invite you to read it through as a whole chapter first, and then we will break down each prophetic declaration Isaiah makes about the Messiah.

> Who has believed our report? And to whom has the arm of the LORD been revealed? For he grew up before Him as a tender plant and as a root out of a dry ground. He has no form or majesty that we should look upon him nor appearance that we should desire him. He was despised and rejected of men, a man of sorrows and acquainted with grief. And we hid, as it were, our faces from him; he was despised, and we did not esteem him. Surely he has borne our grief and carried our sorrows; yet we esteemed him stricken, smitten of God, and afflicted. But he was wounded for our transgressions, he was bruised for our iniquities; the chastisement of our peace was upon him, and by his stripes we are healed. All of us like sheep have gone astray; each of us has turned to his own way, but the LORD has laid on him the iniquity of us all. He was oppressed, and he was afflicted, yet he opened not his mouth; he was brought as a lamb to the slaughter, and as a sheep before its shearers is silent, so he opened not his mouth. By oppression and judgment he was taken away, and who shall declare his generation? For he was cut off out of the land of the living; for the transgression of my people he was struck. His grave was assigned with the wicked, yet with the rich in his death, because he had done no violence, nor was any deceit in his mouth. Yet it pleased the LORD to bruise him; He has put him to grief. If he made himself as an offering for sin, he shall see his offspring, he shall prolong his days, and the good pleasure of the LORD shall prosper in his hand. He shall see of the anguish of his soul and be satisfied. By his knowledge My righteous servant shall justify the many, for he shall bear their iniquities. Therefore, I will divide him a portion with the great, and he shall divide the spoil with the strong, because he poured out his soul to death, and he was numbered with

the transgressors, thus he bore the sin of many and made intercession for the transgressors.

—ISAIAH 53:1–12

THE MESSIAH WAS NOT BELIEVED (v. 1)

"Who has believed our report? And to whom has the arm of the Lord been revealed?"

Right away the prophet alludes to doubt surrounding a "report." If we correctly consider that the rest of this chapter is about the Messiah, then already Isaiah is saying that many will fail to recognize or believe Him when He comes. This was certainly the case with Yeshua. Though massive crowds followed Him and His popularity swelled at times, by the end of Jesus' ministry so had fervent opposition against Him. The religious leaders who plotted His death stirred up enough dissent among the Jews that when given the option of having Jesus or a murdering revolutionary named Barabbas released, the crowd responded almost unanimously: "Crucify Him!" they said of Jesus (Mark 15:13). Clearly they rejected the notion that Jesus was the Messiah.

The "arm of the Lord" Isaiah refers to can mean the Messiah as an extension (or "arm") of the Lord, or it can refer to God's power, which Jesus displayed through miracles. Either way, this "arm" was revealed to humanity, and yet many did not believe. John 1:10–11 says, "He was in the world, and the world was created through Him, yet the world did not know Him. He came to His own, and His own people did not receive Him."

THE MESSIAH WAS GOD'S SON (v. 2)

"For he grew up before Him as a tender plant and as a root out of a dry ground. He has no form or majesty that we should look upon him nor appearance that we should desire him."

The first part of verse 2 presents a huge dilemma for Jewish readers because it alludes to the Father-Son relationship within the Trinity. That may sound like a giant leap in interpretation given a first reading of this verse, but allow me to explain based solely on Isaiah's original text.

If the Messiah "grew up before Him (God)," then that means He was in God's presence. Judaism holds that to be in God's presence, one must be righteous. The Law itself proved that no one but God could be continually righteous, and yet the Messiah would have to be if He grew up before Him. That alludes to a deeper relationship, then, between the Messiah and God—one that sounds consistent with a previous Messianic prophecy Isaiah wrote: "For unto us a child is born, unto us a son is given, and the government shall be upon his shoulder. And his name shall be called Wonderful Counselor, Mighty God, Eternal Father, Prince of Peace" (9:6). It also adds light to other Messianic prophecies that contained elements of a Father-Son relationship, such as Psalm 2:7: "He said to me, 'You are My son; this day have I begotten you.'"

We discussed in chapter 4 why it is so difficult for most Jews to accept the idea of God having a son. Judaism's core belief is that God is one; therefore, any notion of Him being divided is heresy. You can imagine, then, why the idea of the Messiah inherently being God's Son would be equally difficult to accept. Although Judaism has no consensus viewpoint on the Messiah, most Jews generally do not believe the Messiah will be divine. Instead, they believe he will be an "ordinary yet extraordinary" human descended directly from David who will become a great military and political figure and whose leadership skills will be even greater than Moses'—which is as high a compliment as any Jew can give. According to Judaism, the Messiah will rally the Jewish people—and eventually the entire world under his rule—and return them to Torah observance, and out of this will come unprecedented world peace.[4]

Given this, can you see how Isaiah 53:2 creates some major obstacles for a Jew if it is indeed about the Messiah? The notion of an unrecognized Messiah does not fit the traditional Jewish paradigm, despite scriptures such as Isaiah 53 describing Him that way.

We see this concept of Jesus being God in the flesh yet being unrecognized for who He was expressed clearly in John's Gospel. John

1:10–11 says, "He was in the world, and the world was created through Him, yet the world did not know Him. He came to His own, and His own people did not receive Him." Later the disciple points out that "even [Jesus'] brothers did not believe in Him" (7:5). Jesus was fully God and fully man, yet Isaiah describes how out of place He must have felt on earth by saying He was like "a root out of a dry ground" (Isa. 53:2).

Nevertheless, Jesus, the Son of God, "grew up before" the Father while on earth. He was human yet God at the same time, allowing Him to be both in the flesh and constantly righteous before the Father. The Bible says Jesus was and is "in the bosom of the Father" (John 1:18, KJV). He is uncreated and has always been. Yeshua is God in the flesh (John 1:14). He is the visible manifestation of the invisible God (Col. 1:15).

I do not claim to fully understand this mystery or the nature of the Trinity relationship. People try to use different analogies to explain the mystery of the Godhead—the mystery of the relationship between the Father, Son, and Holy Spirit. I have heard some people say it is comparable to the three sections of the egg: the eggshell, the egg white, and the egg yolk. Others use the picture of water taking three forms: solid, liquid, and gas. The funniest one I ever heard was that we could better understand the nature of the Trinity by looking at a Rice Krispies Treat: you get snap, crackle, and pop all in the same bite. These may help some people, but to be honest, they don't help me.

In all seriousness, how can we grasp how God has always been? The human mind can only understand the relationship between things through the law of cause and effect. It is impossible for us to grasp how something came from nothing, and yet this is who God is. Just as we cannot understand the nature of uncreated life, a life form that has no cause, neither should we expect to fathom on this side of glory the mystery of the Trinity. Still the complexity of the Trinity does not negate Isaiah's prophecy about the Messiah, nor does it take away the truth of Jesus as the fulfillment of this verse.

THE MESSIAH DID NOT APPEAR UNUSUAL (v. 2)

"For he grew up before Him as a tender plant and as a root out of a dry ground. He has no form or majesty that we should look upon him nor appearance that we should desire him."

Many who read Isaiah 53 for the first time are surprised by the prophet's mention that Messiah would have nothing in His appearance to make us "desire Him." Most people interpret this to mean Jesus looked plain and unremarkable; others have gone so far as to say it means He was unattractive. We do not know for certain which it is, but what we do know is the shocking statement it makes about God. Jesus was God, the One who formed beauty itself. He designed the northern lights and Mount Everest, the Great Barrier Reef and the Grand Canyon, the Milky Way and Saturn's rings. Simply put, He is the most attractive being in the universe, more stunning and mesmerizing than the mere glimpses of beauty we get in this world. And yet Jesus *willingly* chose to come "clothed" in such mediocrity that nothing about His appearance attracted people to Him. If anyone had a right to flaunt His natural charm, magnetism, and beauty, it was Jesus. And yet Isaiah 52:14, speaking of the cross, says His appearance became "so marred, more than any man, and his form more than the sons of men" that "many were astonished." People were actually disgusted by the fleshly appearance of the God who is beauty itself.

What humility Jesus showed! Some people would even say His way was absurd. If He wanted all people to come to Him, why did He not just display Himself in His true form and draw all men to Himself through His stunning beauty? Why not attract people rather than have them ignore you? The answer, simply put, is because Jesus wants our hearts. He wants us to want Him for Himself. And in His infinite wisdom He knew the best way to do this was to come with "no form or majesty...that we should desire him."

Unfortunately people missed Him because He was so ordinary. Israel was waiting for a superstar—a ten-foot-tall, larger-than-life luminary. Instead, Jesus showed up in such plainness that some "took offense" when they heard rumors of Him claiming to be the Messiah. (See Matthew 13:55–57.) "Who, *that* guy? He's just a carpenter from Nazareth!" they said. "In fact, we know His mom and dad, as well as the rest of the family. They're just like us—normal folk. You seriously think *He's* the Messiah? That's ridiculous! After all, nothing good comes out of Nazareth."

Think about it: Jesus' earthly parents raised Him knowing who He really was: God's Son. I find it hard to believe that they never even dropped a couple of hints to their other sons. So how is it possible Jesus' brothers could have grown up hearing about Jesus' divinity, and yet Scripture says even they did not believe He was the Son of God (John 7:5)? Could it be that Jesus had become *too* ordinary in their eyes?

THE MESSIAH WAS DESPISED, REJECTED, AND FORSAKEN (v. 3)

"He was despised and rejected of men, a man of sorrows and acquainted with grief. And we hid, as it were, our faces from him; he was despised, and we did not esteem him."

People laughed at Jesus for His claims. Some mocked Him openly. The Pharisees made up lies about Him. They and the other religious leaders hated Him so intensely from early on in His ministry that they continually plotted to murder Him (Matt. 26:3–4). So Jesus was well acquainted with being despised, just as He was deeply familiar with sorrow and grief. I wonder if Jesus at times experienced the greatest loneliness a human can possibly feel. Not only was He constantly misunderstood by the public, but His closest friends also seemed clueless as to what He was talking about most of the time.

Yet I wonder which was worse for Jesus: the public vitriol He received from His scoffers, the sorrow He experienced from being misunderstood, or the rejection from those who were His closest friends and family. As I just referenced, Jesus' own brothers did not believe in Him. Worse still, His own disciples, whom He had shared everything with for three years, *all* forsook Him during His worst moments. Though John is mentioned as being present while Jesus hung on the cross, all the other disciples were apparently too afraid for their own lives to stay close (Matt. 26:56). They certainly hid their faces from Him, as Isaiah describes. Peter publicly denied even knowing Jesus three times (Matt. 26:69–75). And of course Judas, whom Jesus trusted enough to handle the group's finances, did not just desert his rabbi but betrayed Him to His death. Just as Isaiah prophesied seven hundred years prior, Jesus knew what it was like to be hated, rejected, despised, and abandoned. He was not just a glorious Savior; He was a sorrowful one too.

THE MESSIAH BORE OUR GRIEF AND SORROWS (v. 4)

"Surely he has borne our grief and carried our sorrows; yet we esteemed him stricken, smitten of God, and afflicted."

Not only would the Messiah be "a man of sorrows and acquainted with grief" (v. 3), but also His purpose would be to bear humanity's sorrow and grief. Jesus was well acquainted with what it felt like to be human. And having experienced firsthand such sorrow and grief (and countless other human emotions and experiences), the Messiah would bear away these things so that we would no longer have to carry them, in the same way an innocent animal sacrificed on the altar under the Law would "bear away" the sins of those who were guilty.

This was exactly Yeshua's purpose. First Peter 2:24 says Jesus "bore our sins in His own body on the tree." Paul expands on this thought, saying, "God made Him who knew no sin to be sin for us, that we might become the righteousness of God in Him" (2 Cor. 5:21). Jesus was sinless and completely innocent, yet He *became* sin itself—bearing our eternal grief and sorrow that would have kept us separated from God—so that we could "become the righteousness of God" and have fellowship with Him once again, just as He originally desired.

Isn't it interesting that those standing at the cross fulfilled the second half of the Messianic prophecy contained in Isaiah 53:4?

As Jesus hung dying, the Roman soldiers, Jewish authorities, and even some among the crowds who had once followed Him all took turns mocking the Lord. Most ridiculed Him by daring Him to save Himself if He really was the Son of God. But without a doubt, those present who mocked Jesus believed that He was being punished by God.

Their assumption was logical; after all, the Torah stated that anyone hanging on a cross was "accursed of God" (Deut. 21:23). Their belief seemed to be confirmed even more when Jesus cried out from the cross, "My God, My God, why have You forsaken Me?" (Matt. 27:46). And yet little did they know that Yeshua HaMashiach was bearing God's punishment for *them* upon Himself. As Paul said, "Christ has redeemed us from the curse of the law by being made a curse for us" (Gal. 3:13). He became the curse itself so that we might not have to be cursed!

Today we may bear some affliction for carrying Jesus' name. As a Jewish person, I have been derided for my choice to follow Jesus. Fellow Jews call me an apostate and think God has cursed me for believing in a false Messiah. Yet I should expect this, just as any believer should expect persecution for their faith. Jesus promised that we would suffer in His name and be "cast out," just as He suffered and was crucified like a criminal outside the holy city of Jerusalem. Hebrews 13:12–13 says, "Therefore Jesus also, so that He might sanctify the people with His own blood, suffered outside the gate. Therefore let us go forth to Him outside the camp, bearing the reproach that He bore."

If we call ourselves followers of Jesus, we should be willing and expect to suffer with Him. Yet 2 Timothy 2:12 reminds us, "If we suffer, we shall also reign with him" (KJV). This is why Jesus said, "Blessed are you when men revile you, and persecute you, and say all kinds of evil against you falsely for My sake" (Matt. 5:11). When we suffer with Jesus, we are in partnership with Him, which is what He has wanted all along and is the very reason He bore our grief and sorrows.

The Messiah Was Wounded
for Our Transgressions (v. 5)

"But he was wounded for our transgressions, he was bruised for our iniquities; the chastisement of our peace was upon him, and by his stripes we are healed."

If you have seen Mel Gibson's *The Passion of the Christ*, then you have a better idea of the physical torture Jesus endured. I am not a proponent of violence in movies, yet I know I am not alone when I say my awareness of what Jesus went through grew by seeing the unimaginable pain He suffered, as so vividly depicted in that film. From the flesh-shredding flogging with a cat-o'-nine-tails to iron spikes ripping into Jesus' hands and feet, the images of His agony were unforgettable. Isaiah speaks of the Messiah being "wounded for our transgressions" and "bruised for our iniquities," yet these words seem to pale when we think of what Jesus actually endured.

As horrific as the Roman soldiers' physical torture was, I do not believe that was what hurt Yeshua the most that day. I believe the greater pain Jesus bore was when He, the sinless One, became sin for us. Yes, Jesus was physically "pierced for our transgressions" (v. 5, NIV), but His perfect heart was also pierced not only with a sensation He had never experienced before—sin—but also with the weight of the sin of the entire world. What was spotless became soiled beyond recognition. If you could imagine the most evil, vile things ever done in human history and multiply that by a thousand, you still would not scratch the surface of what Jesus became that day. The very next verse of Isaiah's Messianic prophecy says, "The LORD has laid on him the iniquity of us all" (53:6). Jesus didn't just carry the weight of the world; He *became* the weight that sends a soul plummeting to the pits of hell.

Because Jesus became sin, the Father had to put Him to death. In His holiness He momentarily turned away from His own Son, which is why Jesus cried out on the cross, "Why have You forsaken Me?" (Matt. 27:46). The separation from His Father was an agony far worse than human flesh could hold.

Keep in mind that Jesus did not just endure such piercing for a theological remedy; He was wounded because of you and me. *Our sin* was what caused Him the greatest pain imaginable.

THE MESSIAH HEALS US BY HIS STRIPES (v. 5)

"But he was wounded for our transgressions, he was bruised for our iniquities; the chastisement of our peace was upon him, and by his stripes we are healed."

The "stripes" Isaiah mentions in this Messianic prophecy were directly fulfilled through Jesus' scourging prior to His crucifixion. When you think about it, the fact that Jesus would endure this in addition to fulfilling many other details surrounding His crucifixion is absolutely remarkable. We do not know exactly how many lashes He received from the Roman torturers, but we can be relatively certain of the instruments they used and the level to which they scourged Jesus. The Romans' objective was to bring a man as close to death as possible without killing him. Yet Isaiah's prophecy says these lashes are the very things that bring about our healing. How can this be? Once again, we find the answer in Jesus as the fulfillment of the Law. Jesus' blood atoned for us in the same way a sacrificial lamb's blood atoned for Israel's sins. How much greater is His blood to bring the ultimate healing!

During Jesus' time on earth supernatural healing was a foundational part of His ministry. He healed wherever He went, and the world had never seen such miraculous power before. From the blood that flowed from His stripes, people are still being healed today— spirit, soul, mind, and body. We often think of healing as a purely physical thing, and yet when Jesus first announced His ministry, He went into the synagogue, opened the scroll, and read the words of Isaiah 61: "The Spirit of the Lord GOD is upon me because the LORD has...sent me to heal the broken-hearted" (v. 1). That was talking about emotional healing!

Isn't it a glorious comfort to realize there is no wounding that we have experienced in life that Jesus cannot heal? Whether a spouse abused you, a friend rejected you at school, a church leader stabbed you in the back, or your parents did not love you growing up—whatever wounding you have experienced, Jesus can completely restore you. By His stripes He offers healing of *every* wound—emotional, physical, and spiritual. Time does not heal all wounds, but Jesus does. Only through Him can we be made whole.

THE MESSIAH DID NOT DEFEND HIMSELF (v. 7)

"He was oppressed, and he was afflicted, yet he opened not his mouth; he was brought as a lamb to the slaughter, and as a sheep before its shearers is silent, so he opened not his mouth."

Isaiah prophesies that the Messiah would face injustice (oppression) and major threats (affliction). He compares the Messiah to an innocent lamb going to its slaughter. Yet twice in one verse the prophet says the Messiah would remain silent in the face of such opposition and attack.

Seven centuries later Jesus fulfilled this prophecy to a tee. Throughout His journey to the cross Jesus remained silent at a time when anyone else would have screamed out in defense or objection. As Mark's Gospel documents, "The chief priests accused Him of many things, but He answered nothing. So Pilate asked Him again, 'Do You answer nothing? See how many things they testify against You.' But Jesus still answered nothing, so that Pilate was astonished" (15:3–5).

Jesus had every right to defend Himself and speak out, yet amid an onslaught of verbal abuse, slander, and vicious lies against Him, He remained cool as a cucumber. He did not try to defend Himself. He did not even respond. Why? Couldn't He have easily pointed out to Pilate how irrational and unfounded the religious leaders' accusations were? Couldn't Jesus have silenced His accusers with a single word?

Yes, He could have. And that was indeed part of the ever-present temptation He faced on His way to the cross. We often say that Jesus could have called upon an army of angels to rescue Him at any moment, and that is correct. He, being God Himself, could have just as easily spoken a single word and shut the mouths of those controlled by irrational, lying, manipulative spirits of evil. This alone shows that Jesus was in complete control throughout His entire death. He lived in victory above it all, and here His supernatural victory was displayed when He did not even respond. He refused to engage with the lying spirits possessing men because He had a greater mission: to save the world. And to do that, He knew He had to endure the suffering of the cross.

THE MESSIAH WAS BURIED IN A RICH MAN'S TOMB (v. 9)

"His grave was assigned with the wicked, yet with the rich in his death, because he had done no violence, nor was any deceit in his mouth."

Some of the prophecies contained in Isaiah 53 are more general and theological in nature (e.g., that He bore our grief and sorrows, or that He was wounded for our transgressions). Yet the prophecy in verse 9 is anything but generic, instead claiming that the Messiah would die "assigned with the wicked," yet He would also be "with the rich." Once again, Yeshua HaMashiach fulfilled this in astounding detail.

First, Jesus was crucified between two criminals. Despite His complete innocence, and despite Pilate calling Jesus a "righteous Man" (Matt. 27:24) and "find[ing] no fault" in Him (Luke 23:4), Jesus was treated as if He had slaughtered a household of children and elderly people. The religious leaders saw Him as worse than a criminal, and they got their way in His punishment. Jesus, therefore, went to His grave "assigned with the wicked," just as Isaiah prophesied (Isa. 53:9).

Second, Isaiah prophesied that the Messiah would be "with the rich in his death," and Yeshua's burial place was literally a gravesite of the wealthy Joseph of Arimathea (Isa. 53:9). Matthew's account describes how accurately this prophecy was fulfilled:

> When the evening came, there came a rich man of Ari-
> mathea, named Joseph, who also was a disciple of Jesus. He
> went to Pilate and asked for the body of Jesus. Then Pilate
> commanded the body to be given to him. When Joseph had
> taken the body, he wrapped it in a clean linen cloth, and
> laid it in his own new tomb, which he had cut out of the
> rock. And he rolled a large stone to the door of the tomb
> and departed.
>
> —MATTHEW 27:57–60

The fact that Pilate *commanded* that Jesus' body be handed over to
Joseph shows something supernatural at work. The intervention of a
Roman governor in a Jewish case such as this was highly unusual. In
addition, notice how Scripture points out that Joseph used his "own
new tomb." Under what kind of situation would anyone give up his
own tomb for another person? I would argue it took divine intervention, which is yet further proof that Jesus is the Messiah.

The Messiah Will Justify Many (v. 11)

"He shall see of the anguish of his soul and be satisfied. By his knowledge My righteous servant shall justify the many, for he shall bear
their iniquities."

On the surface the first statement of this verse—"[God] shall see
the anguish of his soul and be satisfied"—sounds sadistic. Surely the
Father did not enjoy Jesus' suffering, so what was Isaiah prophesying,
and what did he actually mean? The key is in the word *justify*, found
in the next sentence. Essentially verse 11 is all about the substitution-
ary sacrificial death of Yeshua HaMashiach. Although that sounds
complex, it isn't. So let's take a closer look at what it really means.

Do you remember what God's goal was back in the garden with
Adam and Eve? True relationship. He wanted to walk closely with
them. Fast-forward to the Lord's dealings with Moses and the Israelites, and His goal did not change. Through the Law and through
every era during which He spoke through judges, kings, and prophets, God still desired to be close to His people. We already know

from previous chapters that for a guilty person or people to be cleansed, it required the death of an innocent party. So to gain back an unrighteous, sinful people, God required the death of the only righteous person who could "justify" them: His Son, Jesus. Doing this obviously cost Jesus, just as it cost the Father. Both suffered from this requirement. The Father would be separated from His Son, while Jesus would "bear their iniquities," meaning He would literally take on the world's sin (Isa. 53:11).

In light of this, can you understand more what verse 11 actually means when it says God was "satisfied" with the anguish of Jesus' soul? It in no way means God took delight—quite the opposite. The word *satisfy* is used in the same way a judge would be "satisfied" once a prisoner serves his full term, or a collector would be "satisfied" once a bill is completely paid. This was exactly what Jesus did with His death on the cross. Through His anguish He justified— settled the terms of righteousness—all those who would believe. Paul spoke of this wonderful fulfillment in a well-known passage to the Roman believers:

> While we were yet weak, in due time Christ died for the un-godly. Rarely for a righteous man will one die. Yet perhaps for a good man some would even dare to die. But God demonstrates His own love toward us, in that while we were yet sinners, Christ died for us. How much more then, *being now justified by His blood*, shall we be saved from wrath through Him. For if while we were enemies, we were reconciled to God by the death of His Son, how much more, being reconciled, shall we be saved by His life. Furthermore, we also rejoice in God through our Lord Jesus Christ, through whom we have now received reconciliation.
> —ROMANS 5:6–11, EMPHASIS ADDED

THE MESSIAH INTERCEDED FOR TRANSGRESSORS (V. 12)

"Therefore, I will divide him a portion with the great, and he shall divide the spoil with the strong, because he poured out his soul to death, and he was numbered with the transgressors, thus he bore the sin of many and made intercession for the transgressors."

It is far too easy in Christian circles for terms such as *justify* and *reconciliation* to become so well-worn that they lose their meaning. I believe this is also true for the term *intercession*, which unfortunately these days has been relegated in many churches to a term used only by super-spiritual prayer warriors.

Intercession is not a type of prayer. Intercession is a positional state of being that is not just a "Christianese" term but is used in everyday life. Lawyers intercede for their clients before a judge. Negotiators intercede on behalf of companies trying to strike a deal. When Isaiah prophesies in this verse that the Messiah "made intercession for the transgressors," he is referring to the Anointed One standing as a mediator—an intercessor—between a perfect God and those who deserve judgment for their sin (Isa. 53:12).

We have already examined how Jesus did this when He became sin for us and took the full penalty of judgment against sin, which was death. The innocent (Jesus) was punished for the guilty (us) so that the guilty would be redeemed. Can you see how Jesus became our intercessor? He stood before the Father, representing us and making amends on our behalf. While He hung on the cross in complete agony, separated from the Father, even then He made intercession for us when He cried out, "Father, forgive them, for they know not what they do" (Luke 23:34). The power of Jesus' statement extended far past the Roman guards, the Jewish religious leaders, and the crowds who were to blame for His crucifixion. Jesus' words "forgive them" were so powerful that they continue to extend to us today, more than two thousand years later. His forgiveness covers every sin we have committed today, and it will continue to cover His people's sins—always. What power!

Today Jesus "intercedes for us" from His position in heaven as He stands "at the right hand of God" (Rom. 8:34). This does not mean He is up there praying to the Father for us, hoping that the Father will hear us and forgive us. Instead, it means He stands as our constant mediator before the Father. His very presence before the Father means we are always welcome now! Indeed, Jesus has "made intercession" for us for all time.

EXPLAINING ISAIAH

As we conclude this chapter, I hope you share the sense of awe I have whenever I read Isaiah 53. It is a life-changing chapter when our eyes are opened to the reality of who Jesus is and how He fulfills *every* element of Messianic prophecy. In fact, this eye-opening revelation is exactly what happened in the Book of Acts to a foreigner traveling in the middle of a desert.

Acts 8 tells the story of an Ethiopian eunuch who was traveling by chariot from Jerusalem to Gaza. While he sat in his chariot, he read from the Book of Isaiah—specifically the seventh and eighth verses of chapter 53—but did not understand whom the passage was talking about. The apostle Philip had previously been instructed by an angel of the Lord to travel the same way, and when he saw the eunuch passing by, the Holy Spirit instructed Philip, "Go to this chariot and stay with it" (Acts 8:29).

"Then Philip ran to [the eunuch], and heard him read the book of Isaiah the prophet, and said, 'Do you understand what you are reading?' He said, 'How can I, unless someone guides me?' So he invited Philip to come up and sit with him" (vv. 30–31).

Acts 8 says that after the eunuch reread the scripture, he turned and asked Philip, "'I ask you, of whom does the prophet speak, of himself or of someone else?' Then Philip spoke, beginning with the same Scripture, and preached Jesus to him" (vv. 34–35).

It did not take long for the eunuch's eyes to be opened to the revelation of Yeshua HaMashiach. I believe it can be the same way for anyone once they have seen how intricately God has woven Scripture together. So often as believers we see the Old Testament and New Testament as separate books, but God never intended it that way. They are a single story, and the more we recognize how the Tanakh is fulfilled through Jesus, the more the B'rit Hadashah comes to life as a continuation of what God established through "the Law and the Prophets."

As Philip and the eunuch did that, the Ethiopian could not help but respond with action. The story continues:

> As they went on their way, they came to some water. And the eunuch said, "Look, here is water. What hinders me from being baptized?" Philip said, "If you believe with all your heart, you may." He answered, "I believe that Jesus Christ is the Son of God." And he commanded the chariot to halt. Then both Philip and the eunuch went down into the water, and he baptized him. When they came up out of the water, the Spirit of the Lord took Philip away. And the eunuch saw him no more, and he went his way rejoicing.
>
> —ACTS 8:36–39

This is a perfect example of where the revelation of Jesus Christ, as given through Isaiah 53, led to a life changed. I am not sure if the Ethiopian eunuch was the first person to experience this after reading Isaiah's passage, but I am certain he was not the last. I personally know of many others—both Jews and Gentiles—who have come to faith in Yeshua through this passage.

Jesus is the true fulfillment of all that we read in the Old Testament. And in one of the Hebrew Bible's core Messianic prophetic passages, this resonates even more with life-changing power.

CHAPTER 14

THE RESOLUTION

I FREQUENTLY TRAVEL BY air in my ministry, and because of this it has become increasingly important over the years to find whatever shortcuts I can to save time on routing. I am a big fan of direct flights and avoid taking longer, multi-stop routes whenever possible. But even for the most frequent flier, there are still times when you are at the mercy of airlines.

This was the case not too long ago when I made reservations for what should have been an easy trip from Phoenix to Dallas. Given that most airlines fly directly between those cities, I was surprised to find that no direct flights were available for the days I needed to travel. So I took what was available and booked a flight with the shortest layover time possible in between. I figured making my connecting flight in Denver would not be an issue.

I was wrong. First, my flight out of Phoenix was delayed almost an hour due to mechanical issues. When we finally boarded the plane and were ready for takeoff, our plane ended up in queue on the tarmac for another thirty minutes. By the time we departed, I already knew I would miss my connecting flight.

This happens all the time, so I assumed that finding another flight once I landed in Denver would not be a problem. But once again, I was wrong. The weather in Denver that day was absolutely horrible—the once-a-year kind of storm every traveler dreads. Landing amid the strong winds in Denver had already been an adventure; now, as I tried to find another flight to my final destination, I discovered hundreds of other passengers from previous flights were doing the same thing. Gate agents were overwhelmed with rebooking passengers amid the maze of delayed flights, canceled flights, full flights, overbooked flights, misdirected baggage, and gates packed with disgruntled travelers.

I waited two and a half hours at one departure gate, where I was held on standby, only to eventually discover the flight had to be canceled because of the weather. The same was true for my next reassigned flight, where I waited another three hours. By late evening, with planes still grounded and the storm outside still raging, I finally accepted the fact that I would not make a connecting flight. I booked a hotel room to stay in that night and left two days later for home, never having made it to my final destination.

Throughout this book we have addressed the separation between Judaism and Christianity. We have delved into some of the historical and theological reasons for this split. We have also discussed the ramifications as Christianity grew into the world's largest religion and increasingly lost its Jewish roots. I hope you can see by now how the chasm that exists today between these two religions was never God's intent. Jesus came to fulfill the Jewish Law, not to abolish it, yet the Jewish people since the time of Christ have continually rejected Him as Messiah and failed to see how He fulfills the very Scriptures they hold in such high regard. Judaism without Jesus, however, is like never making the flight to Dallas. Judaism without Jesus misses the final destination. It veers far from its ultimate point and purpose. The truth is that Jesus is not just the final destination for the flight; He is the entire *reason* for flying in the first place. The Jewish journey exists to be completed by Jesus, and without that realization the Jewish people will continually be frustrated. Jesus did not come to abolish biblical Judaism; He came to fulfill it.

Centuries of Christian anti-Semitism and unbiblical theology have left Christianity with a church largely sterilized from its Jewish past. In a way, you could say modern-day Christianity is like a flight that reached its final destination—Christ—but has forgotten where it departed from and how it got there. I meet far too many believers who only know a "Christianized" version of Jesus and have never explored the treasures of their Jewish-rooted faith.

Because you have read this book, you are undoubtedly not one of those believers. But whether the information you have discovered in these pages is brand-new to you or simply adds to a faith already well connected to the Hebrew Bible, I pray that you have received new revelation from the Lord through what I have shared. When we search through the deeper truths of the Hebrew Bible and see how it is knit seamlessly with the New Testament, then we will find "new treasures as well as old," just as Jesus promised (Matt. 13:52, NIV).

CREATED FOR RELATIONSHIP

We live in an exciting time in which some of the Tanakh's ancient prophecies are still unfolding. A century ago no one would have ever imagined millions of Jews making *aliyah* and returning to "the Land" from all over the world. The fact that Israel exists is a miracle in itself and a direct fulfillment of Isaiah's ancient prophecy: "Who has heard such a thing? Who has seen such things? Shall the earth be made to give birth in one day? Shall a nation be born at once?" (Isa. 66:8). Indeed, the nation of Israel *was* birthed in a single day, on May 14, 1948. Meanwhile, other Old Testament prophecies continue to be fulfilled in our time, and we are progressively receiving new revelation about those already completed.

Yet no matter how many prophecies are fulfilled or revelations received, the underlying purposes of God remain the same for Jews and Christians alike. He desires a people who will walk closely with Him. He wants devoted disciples, not people who, as in many cases throughout history, use His name merely as a social status. Today the overwhelming majority of people who call themselves Christians live out a nominal faith far from what the Bible describes as following Jesus.

In Revelation 3:20 the Lord says, "Listen! I stand at the door and knock. If anyone hears My voice and opens the door, I will come in and dine with him, and he with Me." Jesus is waiting for us to open our hearts and allow Him to be Lord of our lives. He has already promised that if we allow Him to come in and take up residence as Master, then we will experience a level of fulfillment that we were always made to experience. We were created for relationship with God. We were created to house the very Spirit of God inside us, which Jesus promised to give us when He left this earth. As the Holy Spirit guides us into all Truth—not informational truth but the person called Truth, Jesus—we will then know God more and find our identity in Him.

Beloved, this is the only place we will find real satisfaction and fulfillment. We may chase fulfillment through our careers or money or fame or finding "the one" or a hundred other things. But these things ultimately will not satisfy the deep longing with which each of us was created. Jesus says the only way we can find real fulfillment and life is through Him. He is "the way, the truth, and the life" (John 14:6). And He describes the ultimate, eternal life as this: "That they may know You, the only true God, and Jesus Christ, whom You have sent" (17:3). I am not suggesting that we will feel happy all the time. In fact, I often feel as if I am standing on a battleship that is cutting across the dark ocean at night during war. The truth is that life is a battle. God knew we needed an adversary to become fully mature as His sons and daughters. Still when we come into a relationship and into alignment with our Creator, the One who loves us and created us for Himself, we will enter into the truth of who we are by finding ourselves in Him.

If you do not know Jesus or have never made Him Lord of your life, then I would urge you to do so now. You can put down this book and talk honestly with Him. Pour out your heart to Him; He can handle whatever questions, fears, struggles, or wounds you have. Surrender your life to Him, knowing you are in the hands of the One who loves you more than you could ever imagine and who cares for every part of you. I invite you to pray something like this, using your own words:

> *Jesus, thank You for Your love for me. Thank You for coming to the world and dying for my sins. Thank You for making a way for me to be in relationship with You. I thank You that You did this because You love me, and I receive You*

now into my life. Come, Jesus, live inside me. I make You
Lord of my life. Forgive me for my sins. I want to know You.
Help me repent. Help me love You. Jesus, by Your grace,
I'm asking You now to strengthen me so that from this day
forward I can pick up my cross, deny myself, and follow You.

Maybe you are a believer but you now realize that you have been living for your own purposes. Maybe you have followed Jesus for a long time but allowed your relationship with Him to grow cold. Or maybe you are beginning to see that your view of Jesus has been too narrow. Whatever the case, I encourage you to continue digging deeper into God's Word, asking for His guidance as He reveals more of Himself to you. As you pray for this, know that He is faithful and hears your cry. He is waiting to respond!

A KING RETURNING

In the previous chapter, we took an in-depth look at Isaiah 53, which reveals Jesus the Messiah as the suffering servant. I want to end by now reminding you of the other side of Yeshua HaMashiach.

Did you know that when Jesus returns to earth, He will not come as a giant, soft teddy bear? Did you realize He will not come singing "Kumbaya" as he tiptoes through the tulips? In case you have not read the Book of Revelation or any of the Tanakh's end-times prophecies, let me give you a spoiler alert: Jesus will come in awesome, terrifying power. He will return as history's mightiest warrior and King, and the scene of His return will not be pretty for many. Isaiah is one of many Old Testament prophets who painted a less-than-flowery picture of Jesus' return at Armageddon:

> For the LORD shall come with fire and with His chariots like a whirlwind, to render His anger with fury and His rebuke with flames of fire. For by fire and by His sword on all flesh, the LORD shall execute judgment; and the slain of the LORD shall be many.
> —ISAIAH 66:15–16

Hundreds of years later the apostle John received a similar vision of Jesus' return, and he described this in the Book of Revelation:

> I saw heaven opened. And there was a white horse. He who sat on it is called Faithful and True, and in righteousness He judges and wages war. His eyes are like a flame of fire, and on His head are many crowns....Out of His mouth proceeds a sharp sword, with which He may strike the nations. "He shall rule them with an iron scepter." He treads the winepress of the fury and wrath of God the Almighty. On His robe and on His thigh He has a name written: KING OF KINGS AND LORD OF LORDS. And I saw an angel standing in the sun, and he cried with a loud voice to all the birds flying in the midst of heaven, "Come and gather for the supper of the great God, to eat the flesh of kings, the flesh of commanders, the flesh of strong men, the flesh of horses and their riders, and the flesh of all men, both free and slave, both small and great!"... The remnant were slain with the sword which proceeded out of the mouth of Him who sat on the horse. And all the birds gorged themselves with their flesh.
> —REVELATION 19:11–12, 15–18, 21

What a description! The Lord's return will easily mark the worst day in history for those who refuse to make Jesus their Lord. His might and power will be on full display as He comes to judge the nations. This is why earlier in Revelation, John says, "Look! He is coming with clouds, and every eye will see Him, even those who pierced Him. And all the tribes of the earth will mourn because of Him" (1:7).

Thankfully, however, those who love Jesus and who have put their trust in Him do not have to join in the mourning or even fear for this day. In fact, Isaiah assures us, "Then you shall see this, and your heart shall rejoice, and your bones shall flourish like an herb" (Isa. 66:14). The coming of the Lord will be a day of celebration like none other for believers, as we finally get to see the mighty King of kings and Lord of lords face to face.

A LION ROARING

Yeshua HaMashiach will finally be revealed as the mighty King on this day, silencing all the doubters, cynics, and haters throughout history who claimed He was a mere human imposter. And upon His return Jesus will begin His reign over the entire world as its rightful King. This could not be better news for His people, as Scripture proves He is jealous for us and will rule over us with fierce love, complete justice, wisdom, and peace.

Early in this book I explained why Jesus is called the Lion of Judah. In John's vision of the heavenly throne room, he witnessed Jesus as "the Lion of the tribe of Judah" (Rev. 5:5) and the only One worthy to open the scrolls that bring this present age to an end and usher in a new heavenly reality.

Lions are not teddy bears. As soft as they may look, they can be ferocious and wild. A lion earns its title as king of the jungle for one reason: it is powerful beyond compare. A lion's roar scares off any potential opponents and can be heard from as far as five miles away, reaching a volume of 114 decibels.[1] My point: lions are loud and powerful!

We would be foolish, then, to assume that Jesus was called the Lion of Judah just as a cute nickname. In several places Scripture mentions God roaring over His people in the same way a lion roars over his pride to protect it. Amos 3:8 declares, "The lion has roared; who will not fear? The LORD God has spoken; who can but prophesy?" Hosea says, "The LORD ... roars like a lion. When He roars, His children will come trembling from the west" (11:10). And the prophet Joel gets even more specific with the picture of Jesus roaring over His own: "The LORD roars from Zion, and sounds His voice from Jerusalem, and heaven and earth quake. But the LORD is a refuge for His people, and a stronghold for the children of Israel" (Joel 3:16).

How amazing is it that the same Jesus who silenced Himself

as the suffering servant on the cross and who would not open His mouth against His accusers and torturers will one day roar so loudly that heaven and earth will shake? The Lion of Judah will be heard by all, and even as His beloved children, we would do well to remember this side of our King. As the redeemed of the Lord, we no longer have to fear Him for His wrath or anger, but we should still maintain a healthy, holy fear of God and the Lion of Judah who sits on the throne.

The Lion of Judah is roaring in heaven right now. His spirit is speaking forth in the earth, as Jesus is declaring, "He who has an ear, let him hear what the Spirit says to the churches" (Rev. 3:22). My prayer is that the church today would wake up and realize our kingdom identity, which will always be rooted in Israel. Jesus is the Lion of Judah—He has not lost His Jewishness but instead will forever be identified as a Jew. I pray that more Christians today will begin to understand the fuller meaning of this and explore the Jewish roots of their faith not for the sake of gaining information but to receive the deeper revelation of Jesus Christ as the fulfillment of all things.

I also pray for my fellow Jews around the world to have the blinders removed from their eyes regarding Yeshua HaMashiach and to see Him for who He really is. He is not just some "Christian" savior caricatured on the stained-glass windows of Catholic cathedrals; He is the Lion of Judah who roars over Zion and who will forever be jealous over His chosen people, the Jews. Despite what today separates Christians and Jews, one day we will return to the kingdom identity the Lion of Judah has longed for us to share from the beginning—His people, walking with Him in true relationship.

ABOUT THE AUTHOR

MESSIANIC RABBI K. A. Schneider, a Jewish believer in Jesus and end-times messenger of the Lord, delivers the word of the Lord with a true passion of the Holy Spirit. When Rabbi Schneider was twenty years old, the Lord suddenly awakened him and revealed Himself as Jesus the Messiah on the cross, and his life has never been the same. He has since pastored, traveled internationally as an evangelist, and served as rabbi of a Messianic synagogue.

Rabbi Schneider is the host of the international television broadcast *Discovering the Jewish Jesus*, which can be seen seven days a week in more than one hundred million homes in the United States and approximately two hundred nations worldwide. Viewers tune in regularly as Rabbi Schneider shows with exceptional clarity how the Old and New Testaments connect and how Jesus completes the unfolding plan of God. For a list of times and stations that broadcast Rabbi Schneider's program in your area, visit www.DiscoveringTheJewishJesus.com and click on the "Ways to Watch" tab.

In addition to hosting mass evangelistic crusades and broadcasting through television all around the world, Rabbi Schneider is the author of five books, including *Experiencing the Supernatural*, *The Book of Revelation Decoded*, and *Awakening to Messiah*. He and his wife, Cynthia, have two children.

NOTES

INTRODUCTION: THE LORD IS ONE, SO WHAT HAPPENED TO HIS PEOPLE?

1. Christian Carson, "Beachwood Has the Second-Highest Jewish Population Per Capita Outside Israel," Rebuild Cleveland, March 27, 2014, http://www.rebuildcle.com/2014/03/beachwood -has-second-highest-jewish.html.

2. There are some Jewish people who do speak about having a personal relationship with God, particularly in the ultra-Orthodox Hasidic sects. Unfortunately my observation has been that "they have a zeal for God, but not according to knowledge. For, being ignorant of God's righteousness and seeking to establish their own righteousness, they did not submit to the righteousness of God" (Rom. 10:2–3).

3. "Shema," Judaism 101, accessed May 13, 2018, http://www .jewfaq.org/shemaref.htm.

4. Gregory Tomlin, "Israel Among 'Least Religious' Countries in World," Christian Examiner, April 22, 2015, http://www .christianexaminer.com/article/israel-among-least-religious -countries-in-world/48808.htm; Frank Newport, "2017 Update on Americans and Religion," Gallup, December 22, 2017, http://news .gallup.com/poll/224642/2017-update-americans-religion.aspx; "A Portrait of Jewish Americans," Pew Research Center, October 1, 2013, http://www.pewforum.org/2013/10/01/chapter-4-religious -beliefs-and-practices/.

5. "How Americans Feel About Religious Groups," Pew Research Center, July 16, 2014, http://www.pewforum.org/2014/07/16 /how-americans-feel-about-religious-groups/.

6. Johannes Due Enstad, "Antisemitic Violence in Europe, 2005–2015," Center for Studies of Holocaust and Religious Minorities, June 2017, accessed May 13, 2018, http://www.hlsenteret .no/publikasjoner/digitale-hefter/antisemittisk-vold-i-europa _engelsk_endelig-versjon.pdf; Anti-Defamation League, "ADL Data

Shows Anti-Semitic Incidents Continue Surge in 2017 Compared to 2016," November 2, 2017, https://www.adl.org/news/press-releases /adl-data-shows-anti-semitic-incidents-continue-surge-in-2017 -compared-to-2016.

7. Daniel Boyarin, *Dying for God: Martyrdom and the Making of Christianity and Judaism* (Redwood City, CA: Stanford University Press, 1999), 6; Alan F. Segal, *Rebecca's Children: Judaism and Christianity in the Roman World* (Cambridge, MA: Harvard University Press, 1986), 1.

CHAPTER 2: THE JEWISHNESS OF JESUS

1. Paul Humber, "400 Prophecies of Christ in the Old Testament," Associates for Biblical Research, July 27, 2012, http://www .biblearchaeology.org/post/2012/07/27/400-Prophecies-of-Christ-in -the-Old-Testament.aspx#Article; Alfred Edersheim, *The Life and Times of Jesus the Messiah* (Grand Rapids, MI: Christian Classics Ethereal Library, 1953), accessed February 15, 2018, http://www .ntslibrary.com/PDF%20Books/The%20Life%20and%20Times%20 of%20Jesus%20the%20Messiah.pdf.

2. Conrad Hackett and David McClendon, "Christians Remain World's Largest Religious Group, but They Are Declining in Europe," Pew Research Center, April, 5, 2017, http://www.pewresearch .org/fact-tank/2017/04/05/christians-remain-worlds-largest-religious -group-but-they-are-declining-in-europe/.

3. Hackett and McClendon, "Christians Remain World's Largest Religious Group, but They Are Declining in Europe."

4. Ray Vander Laan, "Rabbi and Talmidim," accessed May 14, 2018, https://www.thattheworldmayknow.com/rabbi-and-talmidim; Trent C. Butler, ed., s.v. "Education in Bible Times," Holman Bible Dictionary, accessed May 14, 2018, https://www.studylight.org /dictionaries/hbd/e/education-in-bible-times.html.

5. Vander Laan, "Rabbi and Talmidim."

CHAPTER 3: JEALOUSY

1. Steven B. Most, J. P. Laurenceau, E. Graber, A. Belcher, and C. V. Smith, "Blind Jealousy? Romantic Insecurity Increases Emotion-Induced Failures of Visual Perception," *Emotion* 10, no. 2 (2010): 250–256.

2. Jeanna Bryner, "Jealousy Really Is Blinding, Study Finds," Live Science, April 14, 2010, https://www.livescience.com/10986-jealousy -blinding-study-finds.html.

3. Shemuel Safrai and M. Stern, eds., *The Jewish People in the First Century: Historical Geography, Political History, Social, Cultural and Religious Life and Institutions*, vol. 2 (Leiden, Netherlands, Brill Academic, 1974), 600–612.

4. Joseph Telushkin, "Ancient Jewish History: The Great Revolt," Jewish Literacy (New York: William Morrow and Co., 1991), accessed May 15, 2018, http://www.jewishvirtuallibrary.org/the-great -revolt-66-70-ce.

5. David Gurevich, "Why Did Vespasian and Titus Destroy Jerusalem? The Roman Political Perspective on the Destruction of the City," TheTorah.com, accessed May 15, 2018, http://thetorah.com /why-did-vespasian-and-titus-destroy-jerusalem/; Telushkin, "Ancient Jewish History."

6. Telushkin, "Ancient Jewish History."

7. Telushkin, "Ancient Jewish History."

8. Telushkin, "Ancient Jewish History."

9. Telushkin, "Ancient Jewish History."

10. Peter Shirokov and Eli Lizorkin-Eyzenberg, "Council of Jamnia and Old Testament Canon," Israel Institute of Biblical Studies, March 8, 2014, https://blog.israelbiblicalstudies.com/jewish-studies /jamnia/.

CHAPTER 4: THEOLOGICAL CRISIS

1. Alison Millington, "Six Common People Who Have Claimed to Be Royal," Business Insider Nordic, March 9, 2017, http://nordic .businessinsider.com/people-who-have-claimed-to-be-royal-2017-3 ?r=UK&IR=T; Andrea Morabito, "Meet the Maryland Man Who Became a King," *New York Post*, September 8, 2015, https://nypost .com/2015/09/08/meet-the-maryland-man-who-became-a-king/; Laura Rosenfeld, "How Are the Howes Royal? The 'Suddenly Royal' Family Isn't Official Quite Yet," Bustle, September 16, 2015, https:// www.bustle.com/articles/110730-how-are-the-howes-royal-the -suddenly-royal-family-isnt-official-quite-yet.

2. "IoM 'King of Mann' Announces Abdication Online," ITV, March 13, 2017, http://www.itv.com/news/granada/2017-03-13/iom -king-of-mann-announces-abdication-online/.

3. Erica Tempesta, "From Blue-Collar to Blue-Blooded! Mechanic Discovers He Is Heir to the Throne of the Isle of Man After Researching His Ancestry Online—and Travels 3,000 Miles to Claim His Title," *Daily Mail*, August 6, 2015, http://www.dailymail .co.uk/femail/article-3186977/Mechanic-discovers-heir-throne-Isle -Man-researching-ancestry-online-travels-3-000-miles-claim-title .html.

4. Eusebius, *The Church History*, trans. Paul L. Maier (Grand Rapids, MI: Kregel Academic and Professional, 2007), iii, 36.

CHAPTER 5: THE CHANGING LAW

1. Joseph Telushkin, "Judaism: The Oral Law—Talmud and Mishna," Jewish Literacy (New York: William Morrow and Co., 1991), accessed May 21, 2018, http://www.jewishvirtuallibrary.org /the-oral-law-talmud-and-mishna.

2. Telushkin, "Judaism."

3. Yehuda Shurpin, "What Is the Talmud?" Chabad.org, accessed May 21, 2018, https://www.chabad.org/library/article_cdo /aid/3347866/jewish/What-Is-the-Talmud.htm.

4. Felix Just, "'The Jews' in the Fourth Gospel," Catholic -resources.org, accessed June 1, 2018, http://catholic-resources.org /John/Themes-Jews.htm; Willard M. Swartley, "'The Jews' (in the Gospel of John)," AnabaptistWiki.org, September 28, 2015, http:// www.anabaptistwiki.org/mediawiki/index.php?title="The_Jews" _(in_the_Gospel_of_John.

5. Daniel J. Harrington, *John's Thought and Theology: An Introduction* (Collegeville, MN: Liturgical Press, 1990), 26.

6. R. Alan Culpepper, "The Gospel of John as a Document of Faith in a Pluralistic Culture," in *What Is John? Readers and Readings of the Fourth Gospel*, ed. Fernando F. Segovia (Atlanta: Scholars Press, 1996), 115.

7. "Antisemitism in History: From the Early Church to 1400," United States Holocaust Memorial Museum, accessed May 21, 2018, https://www.ushmm.org/wlc/en/article.php?ModuleId=10007170.

8. Eli Lizorkin-Eyzenberg, "Who Are 'the Jews' in the Gospel of John?" Israel Institute of Biblical Studies, November 7, 2012, https://blog.israelbiblicalstudies.com/jewish-studies/who-are-the-jews-in-the-gospel-of-john/.

9. Mark Galli and Ted Olsen, eds., *131 Christians Everyone Should Know* (Nashville, TN: Broadman and Holman Publishers, 2000), 83–86.

10. John Chrysostom, "Against the Jews: Homily I," Tertullian.org, accessed May 21, 2018, http://www.tertullian.org/fathers/chrysostom_adversus_judaeos_01_homily1.htm.

11. Bernard N. Howard, "Luther's Jewish Problem," The Gospel Coalition, October 19, 2017, https://www.thegospelcoalition.org/article/luthers-jewish-problem/.

12. Verónica Zaragovia, "Amid Celebrations of Martin Luther, Some Want to Talk About His Anti-Semitism," *Tablet*, October 31, 2017, http://www.tabletmag.com/jewish-life-and-religion/247747/martin-luther-anti-semitism.

Chapter 6: Inclusion of the Gentiles

1. "What Were Early Christians Like?," Christianity.com, April 28, 2010, https://www.christianity.com/church/church-history/timeline/1-300/what-were-early-christians-like-11629560.html.

2. Grant R. Osborne, ed., "Galatians 2:12—Peter's Separation From Gentile Christians," *The IVP New Testament Commentary Series* (Westmont, IL: IVP Academic, 2010).

3. Fred Skolnik, ed., "Birkat Ha-Minim," *Encyclopaedia Judaica*, second ed. (Farmington Hills, MI: Thomson Gale, 2008), accessed May 21, 2018, https://www.jewishvirtuallibrary.org/birkat-ha-minim.

4. S. Schechter, "Genizah Specimens," *Jewish Quarterly Review* OS 10 (1898), 657; Skolnik, "Birkat Ha-Minim."

5. Steven T. Katz, ed., *The Cambridge History of Judaism: Volume 4, The Late Roman-Rabbinic Period* (New York: Cambridge University Press, 2006), 291.

6. Ruth Langer, *Cursing the Christians? A History of the Birkat HaMinim* (New York: Oxford University Press, 2012), 31–34.

7. Katz, *The Cambridge History of Judaism*, 291.

Chapter 7: The Revolts

1. Richard Gottheil and Samuel Krauss, "Fiscus Judaicus," Jewish Encyclopedia.com, accessed May 21, 2018, http://jewish encyclopedia.com/articles/6157-fiscus-judaicus.

2. Marius Heemstra, *The Fiscus Judaicus and the Parting of the Ways* (Tübingen, Germany: Mohr Siebeck, 2010), 24.

3. Heemstra, *The Fiscus Judaicus and the Parting of the Ways*, 36.

4. Heemstra, *The Fiscus Judaicus and the Parting of the Ways*, 28.

5. J. Louis Martyn, *History and Theology in the Fourth Gospel*, 3rd ed. (Louisville, KY: Westminster John Knox Press, 2003), 56; Raymond E. Brown, *The Gospel According to John I–XII*, Anchor Bible Series, vol. 29 (Garden City, NY: Anchor Bible, 1966), LXX– LXXV, LXXXV.

6. Martyn, *History and Theology in the Fourth Gospel*, 63.

7. Skolnik, "Birkat Ha-Minim."

8. "Ancient Jewish History: The Bar-Kokhba Revolt," Jewish Virtual Library, accessed May 21, 2018, http://www.jewishvirtuallibrary .org/the-bar-kokhba-revolt-132-135-ce.

9. "Ancient Jewish History," Jewish Virtual Library.

10. "Shimon Bar-Kokhba," Jewish Virtual Library, accessed May 21, 2018, http://www.jewishvirtuallibrary.org/shimon-bar-kokhba.

11. Elizabeth Speller, *Following Hadrian: A Second-Century Journey Through the Roman Empire* (Oxford, England: Oxford University Press, 2004), 218.

12. Eusebius Pamphilius, *Eusebius Pamphilius: Church History, Life of Constantine the Great, Oration in Praise of Constantine* (New York: Christian Literature Company, 1890), 803.

13. "Constantine Sees a Vision of the Cross," History Channel, accessed May 21, 2018, https://www.historychannel.com.au/this-day -in-history/constantine-sees-a-vision-of-the-cross/.

14. Pamphilius, *Eusebius Pamphilius: Church History*, 928.

15. "Emperor Constantine and the Jews," Jewish Currents, February 26, 2018, http://jewishcurrents.org/emperor-constantine-and-the -jews/.

Chapter 8: The Nature of God

1. Bible Study Tools, s.v. "*Qodesh*," accessed March 6, 2018, https://www.biblestudytools.com/lexicons/hebrew/nas/qodesh.html.

2. Matt Slick, "Deuteronomy 9:13–14, 'Let Me Alone That I May Destroy Them,'" Christian Apologetics and Research Ministry, accessed March 6, 2018, https://carm.org/deuteronomy-913-14-let-me -alone-i-may-destroy-them.

CHAPTER 10: THE PURPOSE OF THE LAW

1. Yvette Alt Miller, "10 Ideas Judaism Gave the World," Aish .com, August 22, 2016, www.aish.com/sp/ph/10-Ideas-Judaism-Gave -the-World.html?mobile=yes.

CHAPTER 13: ANCIENT PROPHECIES

1. Humber, "400 Prophecies of Christ in the Old Testament"; Edersheim, *The Life and Times of Jesus the Messiah*.

2. Michael L. Brown, *Answering Jewish Objections to Jesus, Volume 3: Messianic Prophecy Objections* (Grand Rapids, MI: Baker Books, 2003), 49–50.

3. C. G. Montefiore and H. Loewe, eds., *A Rabbinic Anthology* (New York: Schocken Books, 1974), 544.

4. Nissan Dovid Dubov, "What Is the Jewish Belief About Moshiach (Messiah)?" Chabad.org, accessed May 24, 2018, https:// www.chabad.org/library/article_cdo/aid/108400/jewish/The-End -of-Days.htm.

CHAPTER 14: THE RESOLUTION

1. Sarah Zielinski, "Secrets of a Lion's Roar," Smithsonian.com, November 3, 2011, https://www.smithsonianmag.com/science -nature/secrets-of-a-lions-roar-126395997/.